MATT WIMAN   SPENCER FISHER   JOHN ALE____
REI ARLOVSKI   EDDIE RUIZ   MATT LINDLAND   GENKI SUDO
MARVIN EASTMAN   FRANK MIR   STEVE BYRNES

ARISYAN   JEFF CURRAN   CHRIS LYTLE ____   RO COR
_E   MIKE BROWN   NICK DIAZ   TIM SYLVIA   JOHN HALV
OCK   TREVOR PRANGLEY   CURTIS STOUT   ROBBIE LAWLEF
TERRELL   JOE DOERKSEN   JON FITCH   JOE RIGGS
D EVANS   YVES EDWARDS   VERNON WHITE   WADE SHI
HALLMAN   JOE STEVENSON   DOKONJONOSUKE MI
CK   GILBERT ALDANA   CHEICK KONGO   CARMELO MARRER
HALES LEITES   RICH FRANKLIN   JAMIE VARNER
PETE SELL   SCOTT SMITH   RICH CLEMENTI   TYSON GRIFFIN
EDWIN DEWEES   KENNY FLORIAN   HECTOR RAMI
HOMAS   JAMES IRVIN   JASON MACDONALD   KEITH JARDINE
ATT HAMILL   EDDIE SANCHEZ   MICHAEL BISPING
PENN   LUIGI FIORAVANTI   BROCK LARSON   DAVE MENNE
_   ALAN BELCHER   JEFF JOSLIN   MATT SERRA   NAT
IEL GONZAGA   ANTONI HARDONK   JOSH SHOCKMAN
RCUS DAVIS   VICTOR VALIMAKI   SHONIE CARTER   DAVID HE
GLEISON TIBAU   JEFF MONSON   DREW FICKETT   TONY DESO

Dedicated to my wife, Hillary, and my son, Luca.

OCTAGON

::

KEVIN LYNCH

Introduction by Lorenzo Fertitta

Foreword by David Mamet

Essay by Dave Hickey

Afterword by Dana White

INTRODUCTION

When my partners and I formed Zuff a , LLC and bought the Ultimate Fighting Championship® in 2001, we invested in a brand and a sport that were under siege. Booted off cable television, mixed martial arts was labeled as barbaric, and the athletes who competed in the events were seen as nothing more than barroom brawlers.

But as fans of the sport and practitioners of martial arts, we had gotten to know some of the athletes and we knew how wrong the detractors were. So our goal was simple: not only were we going to put on great events and entertain fight fans, we were also going to break down barriers. We would let the world know that the people who competed in this sport weren't thugs, but in fact were well-trained and highly educated world-class athletes, ones who participated in this sport for any number of different reasons but who all shared one common bond: the will to compete.

A concept like that is easy to put into words on paper, but some things can only be expressed visually. Sometimes seeing is truly believing. That's why you have this book in your hands right now.

Octagon™ is a project that I have been closely involved with since its inception, and in the time since I first saw the artistry that Kevin Lynch brought to the table, it has taken on a life of its own, one that I'm very proud of.

Kevin has taken the tools of his trade and treated this sport with the respect and love that I have always had for it; he has gotten to the core of what the Ultimate Fighting Championship and its fighters are all about. And though it may sound odd to say, when it comes to the photos you're about to see, it's not always about fighting.

These photos, whether action or still shots, reflect drama, emotion, the heart and soul of what it takes to be a professional athlete in a sport that can leave you a completely different person, be it physically, financially, or emotionally. That drama is the main reason why the before and after photos Kevin has assembled are so compelling. As an active art collector, I can say these are some of the best art photos I have ever seen.

That's because a look into the eyes of each fighter before and after a fight tells a story. Before the fight, you can see whether he's confident, if he's trained properly, and if he's nervous or scared. And while the bruises and cuts may tell a different story after the fight, once again, the eyes give everything away. A fighter may have finally achieved his dream of winning a world championship, or could have been the one losing that title, or may have just won his first fight in the UFC®, a dream held at one time or another by every athlete to ever compete in the sport.

It's moments like these that make finally holding this book in my hands so fulfilling. It's a breakthrough on so many levels, because it allows people to see this sport in a new way. It's visceral, yet understated; in your face, but also containing levels of complexity that are only appreciated after several viewings.

In fact, *Octagon* is like mixed martial arts itself.

LORENZO FERTITTA

FOREWORD

There is a feeling in the serious gym, one like that backstage at an old theater, or inside of a synagogue or church. Like all of them, the gym, the dojo, the Jiu-Jitsu academy has been infused with spirit. It can't be explained or documented, but it is real. It is the legacy of human beings who have striven to perfect themselves.

Fighters are students. They pursue their education in the gym, on the mat, in the Octagon™. Their ancient philosophic school is formally called Stoicism. The Stoics wrote that their philosophy could be reduced to this: hate only those things it is within your power to avoid, desire only that which you have the power to award yourself.

Perhaps one cannot avoid fear, but one can avoid cowardice; one cannot avoid fatigue, but one may refuse to surrender.

There has been a lot of bilge written in this late age about emotions. Emotions, a school of thought holds, are not only good, but indeed are magic. To withhold them causes illness; to express them brings health. But the fighter trains to do the opposite, to force not only his body, but his mind to disregard emotions and obey the will. His model of perfection is not a man immune to defeat, but one immune to the desire to accept his own imperfections.

One wants to be around the fighters. They are involved in a mystery.

DAVID MAMET

I want to talk about fighting, specifically about fighting as a public performance, but the best and most urgent, aspects of this endeavor, I fear, cannot be written about, and the fact that they can't be written about is probably why we fight and watch the fights. What does one say about the exotic, endorphin-fueled rush of pain and pleasure that accompanies ritualized, hard training except that it is real and that it transcends verbal expression. What does one say about the ease of camaraderie among one's peers, about the comfort of stepping into the one place in the world where you know exactly what to do, about the odd gratitude you feel toward your opponent for simply being there, for affording you the opportunity to be brave and fierce. What does one say about the parts that are beyond knowing, like the tumbling, dreamy, virtually painless pain of really being hurt (a feeling that fighters share with surfers) or about the sharp, short burst of exaltation that accompanies victory, then quickly fades and drives the need to fight again.

All these conditions exist but they resist words and they are, in fact, a cure for words, so I want to begin on a broader field with all the lonely arts that aspire to passion and precision, ferocity and nuance, where the risks are great and the truest rewards are spiritual and social--the state of one's heart and the sustenance of one's comrades. In taking the privilege of writing about fighting across boundaries, I am joining a long line of writers better than I: Ernest Hemingway, A. J. Liebling, Norman Mailer, F.X Toole and, most prominently, in this case, Jim Sheridan who began his quest for something real by studying painting at Harvard College, and ended up as the bard of Ultimate Fighting, the poet laureate of all those tattooed hard guys--"the disenfranchised burning to test their manhood, angry at their fathers, the situation, or *something.*"

Many fighters and athletes, of course, end up as artists--eye-hand coordination being the link between them, but Sheridan's taking it the other way, from art to fighting, is a sign of the times, I think, a measure of the anger and desperation that pervades the moment. So let me remind you, here, that the last hundred years have been marked by the greatest flourishing of the temporal arts, fine and martial, in the history of man. The mastery and popularity of these arts has increased exponentially. Now, more than ever, we esteem the arts in which years of training and failure redeem themselves in one blazing, evanescent, improvisational moment of triumph--all those arts, in other words, that are worth going to see on the chance that something magic might transpire. So we are living through a great age of disciplined improvisation--of fighting, dancing, painting, acting, skateboarding and all the rest--of making music, making people laugh, and making love.

Three primary cultural conditions have made this flourishing possible. First, for more than a century, we have been able to *record* those moments that, in previous centuries, melted into the air. The glories of Bel Canto singing, Edmund Kean's acting, and Nijinski's "Rite of Spring," were acclaimed but lost and totally unavailable a few seconds later. Now we have it down to learn from. Second, we still have the right, in this culture, to put ourselves in harm's way and the privilege of not dying in the effort. Finally, we live in a culture in which "the rules" are flexible, easily changeable when they become oppressive, divisive, or boring, and this is good because any time two men fight and both survive the reason is the rules.

Recordings of the improvisational arts are critical, of course. If there were no recordings of Louis Armstrong playing the trumpet, Dixieland jazz would have persisted, but as a kind of folk music. There would be no escalating platform of refinement and innovation—no Bix, no Diz, no Bird, no Trane, no Miles--and, in fact, no Jackson Pollock, either. If there were no films of Jack Johnson and Jack Dempsy, we would still fight but without the innovations and refinements of Sugar Ray Robinson, Rocky Graziano, and Mohammad Ali. There would be no giants upon whose shoulders we might stand. The darker side of our access to representations, of course, resides in their ability to replace the real thing, as video games do, relocating our hearts in our thumbs, but this vice never quite triumphs. The Gods of genetics always throw up wild souls who want to make it real and make it better, so for many young fighters, fighting replaces the video-games of their youth, and in their fighting one can see moves that derive from those games as well as the idea of "levels" in Ultimate Fighting--the fight in the air and the fight on the ground.

The other dark consequence of recorded improvisation is that the explosion of recordings and films offers a profusion of improvisational choices, and these choices we make, create schools of fighting, music, dance, and art. These choices create coteries, specialists, and imitators; they generate infinite divisions and subdivisions. This abundance of niches presents aspirants with self-limiting decisions: Sugar Ray, Bruce Lee, or Royce Gracie? Jackson Pollock, Andy Warhol, or Richard Serra? Bix, Diz, or Chet? Conversations about these competing schools descend into adolescent arguments about "special powers:" Could Captain Marvel beat Superman? Which X-Man would win in a fight between all of them? At this point, the tradition of learning by watching, listening, and reenacting that once set us free becomes a kind of tyranny--precision overwhelms passion, nuance overwhelms ferocity, and greed overwhelms justice.

All we want is a fair fight--something just and beautiful--and this is where the privileges of democracy come into play, because the founding fathers did it right. During the arguments that surrounded the ratification of the American constitution, there were those who argued against a permanent legislature. Why not just make some laws and enforce them forever? For once Alexander Hamilton and Thomas Jefferson agreed: We need lawmakers because we always need new rules, because the needs and desires of commercial cultures change. The rule that liberates us today may easily imprison us tomorrow. The rule that unites us today may easily divide us tomorrow, so the rules change and in the process: they free us from tyranny, divide us according to our preference then reunite us according to our desires. Since the Roman Republic, all the arts, fine and martial, have undergone periods of innovation, periods of division and periods of unification.

In its amazing triumph, however, Mixed Martial Arts, as a unifying discipline, has done something more radical and more global. The traditions of fighting it unifies and the divisions it breaks down are thousands of years old with roots in the gene pools of a thousand cultures: in the folk histories of the Greek and Roman West, of the Gothic north, in the traditions of China, Japan, and Thailand. The fact that all these rich disciplines with deep local roots could proliferate worldwide is a testament to the combative appetite of mercantile capitalism. The fact that all these disciplines could come together in mixed martial arts is a tribute to creative power of cosmopolitanism, to the forces of globalism at their best, to the challenges that face an autumnal America and the ambience of social anger at its darkest.

So people are getting ready for something, they know not what, and, as a consequence, Ultimate Fighting is not ultimate because it lacks rules. It is ultimate because it lacks respite. It goes on tumultuously, non-stop in five-minute rounds (three or five) until a fighter is knocked out or submits. So, it is not the danger and cruelty of the conflict that makes it ultimate but the outrageous demands it places on the body of the fighter. There are rules, in fact, thirty-one of them, designed to make a concussion and bone injury much less likely. Head butting, eye gouging, fish hooking, biting, hair pulling, cursing, spitting, stomping, spiking, clawing, pinching are all verboten. Attacks to the groin, the throat, the fingers and toes, strikes to the back of the head and to the spine are forbidden.

There are rules that accommodate the differing conditions of fighting standing or on the ground. There are rules that eliminate false theater of wrestling (no holding to the enclosure; no throwing your opponent out of the enclosure), and no holds or blows, which, if not rehearsed and expected (as they are in wrestling) would kill. There are rules that eliminate the leisurely politesse of boxing, no broken clinches or standing eights, none of the little rest stops that relax the demands of combat on the body. There are also built-in restraints. Decisive arm, leg, or choke holds that could, if executed decisively, break an arm or a leg are applied gradually to create submissions. The light gloves that allow grappling also encourage tact in blows to the head (the head being harder than the hand in every case). The possibility of grabbing mitigates the boxing and karate moves that require radical extension of the arms or the legs. This also lessens, although it does not eliminate, the advantage of reach.

In the end then, we have, what at the moment, we call a fair fight of immense complexity, one that, quite literally, favors the survival of the fittest, a fight that teaches us things we never quite realized about the lives we live. To take an instance, when I first began watching Ultimate Fighting, I thought the fight on the ground was boring. Gradually it revealed itself to me in all its subtle urgency and one night I realized that this fight, the fight on the ground, is the true metaphor of how we live today. We rarely have the opportunity of stand up and punch it out. On the job, in the office, in the bureaucracy and in the institution we grapple forever on the ground, seeking tiny advantages, bits of leverage and the occasional clean shot. Herein lies the true satisfaction of the standing knockout.

This, I think, is also the key to the question: Why this kind of fight now? I attribute it to the enormous tectonic forces alive in America today, where we have never been so safe or in so much peril. We live in a soup of perfectly interconnected safety with helmet laws, seatbelts, infant seating, low cholesterol, no smoking signs, play-dates, cell-phones, and Blackberries. All this protection coddles those of us who work while we try to survive on the precipice of absolute disaster, without a net. One merger, one outsourced job, one bad decision, one deceptive mortgage, one religious idiot, one accident, illness or sudden death and we are falling forever, and we can't even scream lest we disturb the peace. So you ask: Why fight? I say, Why not? Don't we need a little space, an octagon, perhaps, where we know exactly what's going down?

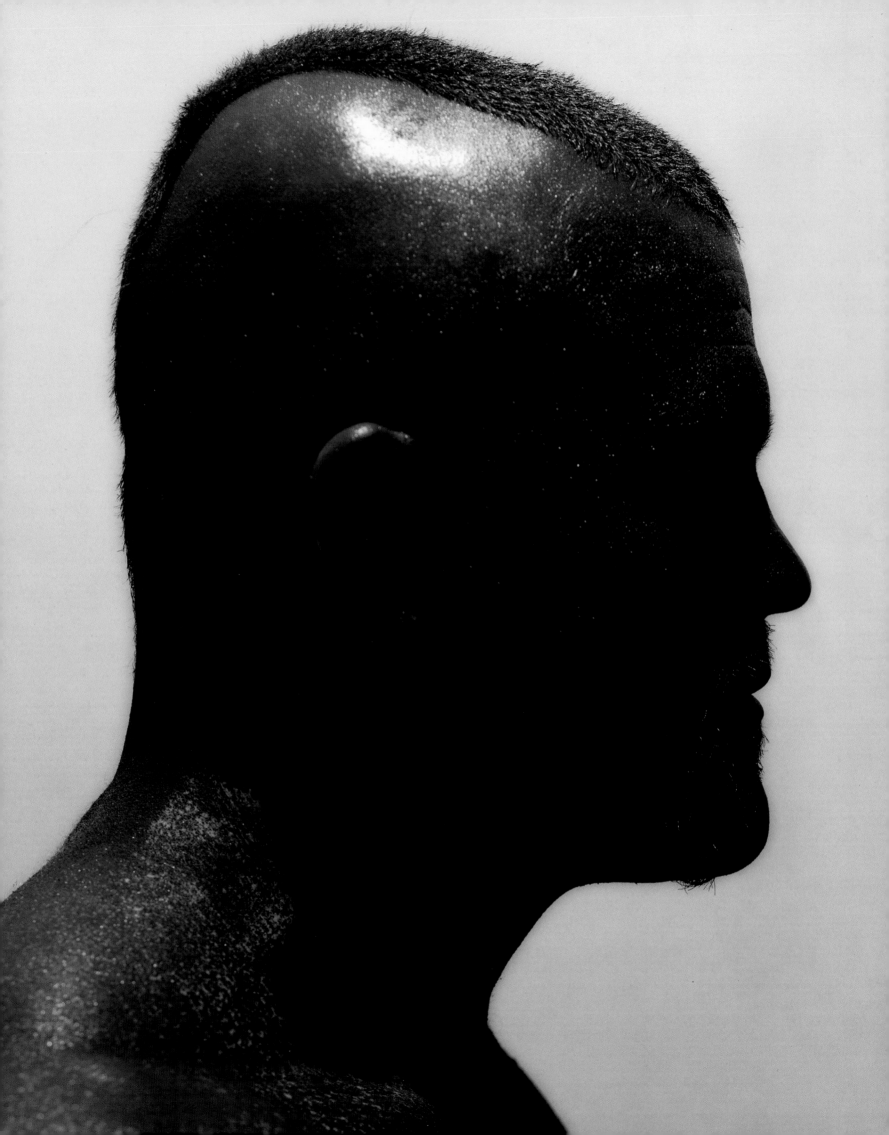

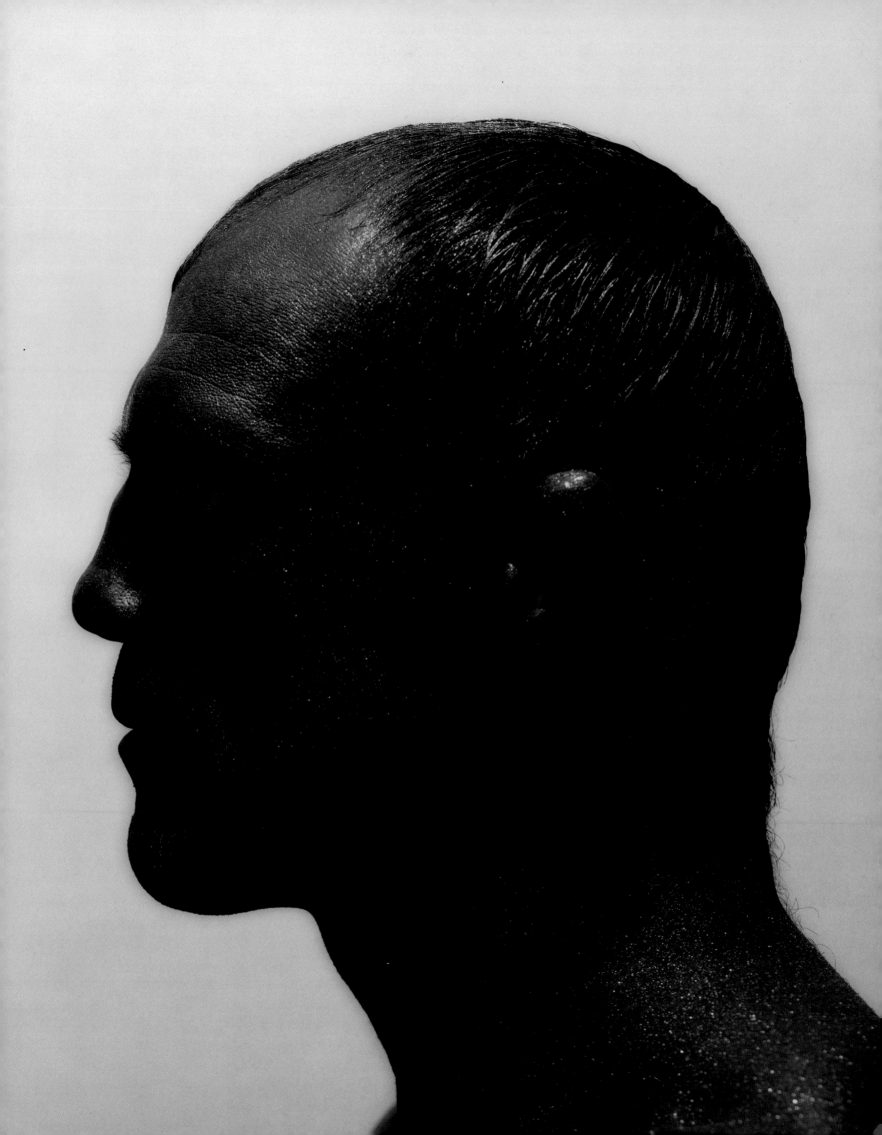

The fact of the matter is that he is going into this fight actually thinking that he can beat me—that gets me more motivated than anything else. Just to think that this man is coming into my Octagon and is actually thinking that he can beat me one-on-one in front of the whole viewing world. That's my big motivation. That's what's running through my mind when I walk to the Octagon and I get up in there, that this guy actually thinks that he's going to beat me.

MATT HUGHES

I think the reason people like me is because I'll fight anybody, anywhere, I don't talk bad about people that don't deserve it, and I'm not a guy who's out there trying to trash talk and make a name for myself. I earned the name that I have—I went out and fought for it.

CHUCK LIDDELL

Honor is not about winning—honor is about you stepping up and standing for what you believe in, and that's it. That's what I do—if somebody says something to me or does something to me, I will stand up.

KEN SHAMROCK

i see dead people...

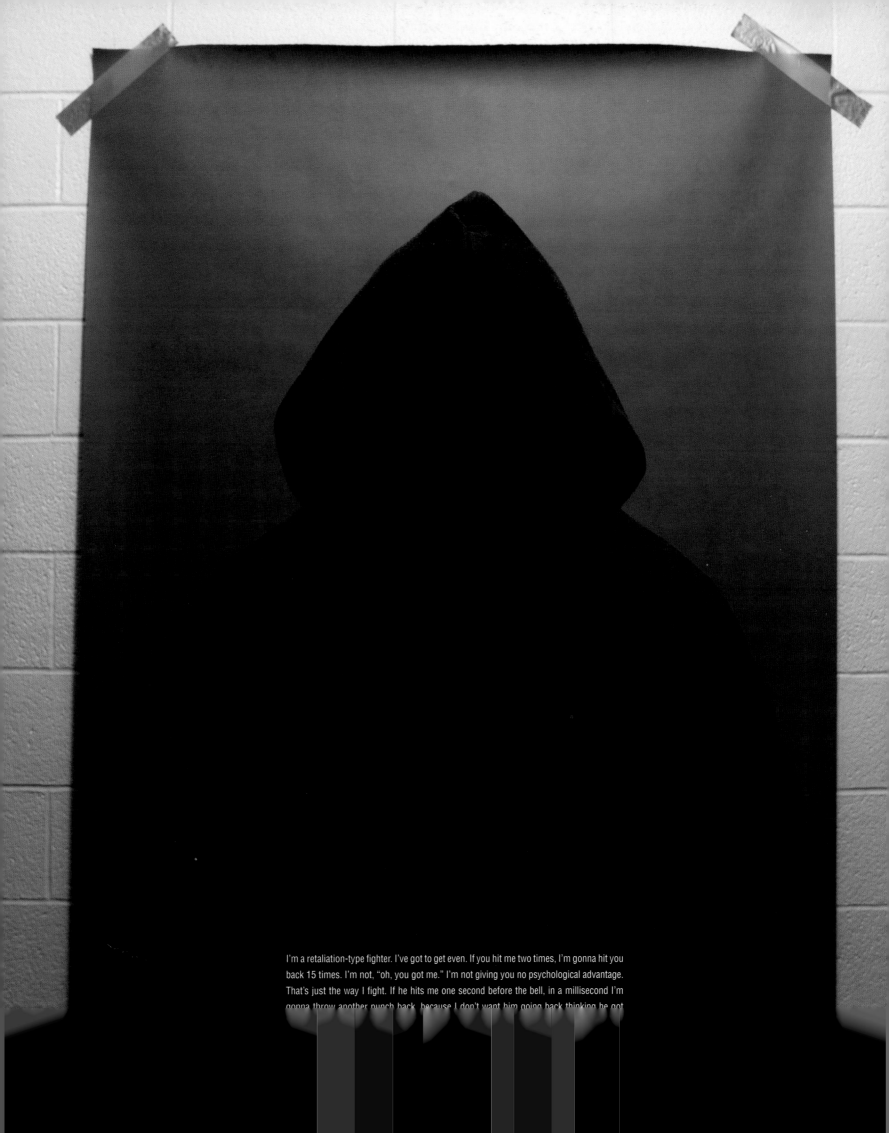

I'm a retaliation-type fighter. I've got to get even. If you hit me two times, I'm gonna hit you back 15 times. I'm not, "oh, you got me." I'm not giving you no psychological advantage. That's just the way I fight. If he hits me one second before the bell, in a millisecond I'm gonna throw another punch back, because I don't want him going back thinking he got

The minute I engage and we're within hand distance, I'm thinking about finishing you—
because the only way I can secure my own safety is if you're unconscious on the ground.
That's just my mentality about it.

FRANK MIR

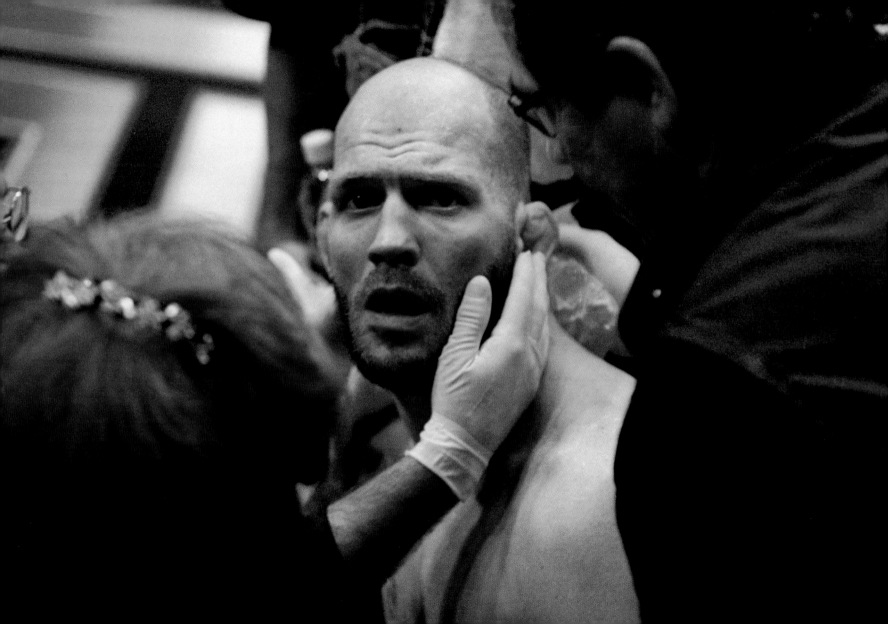

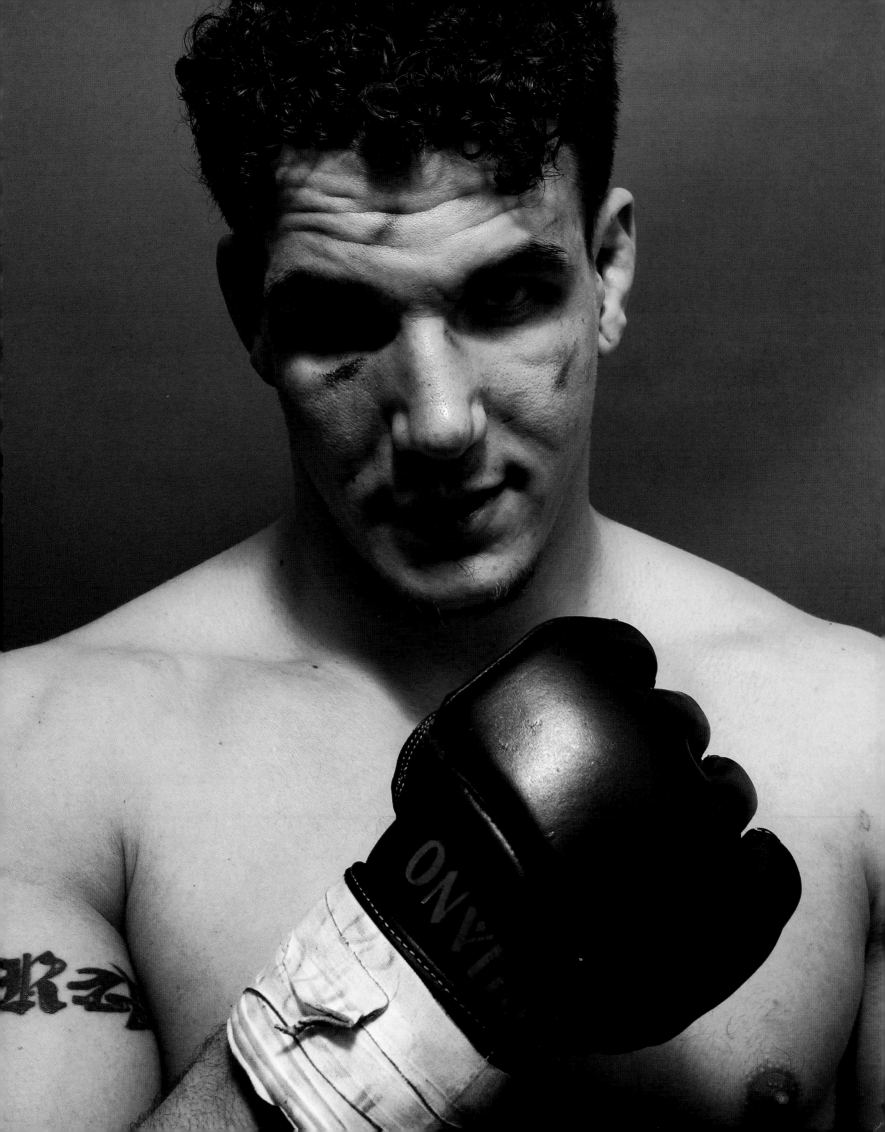

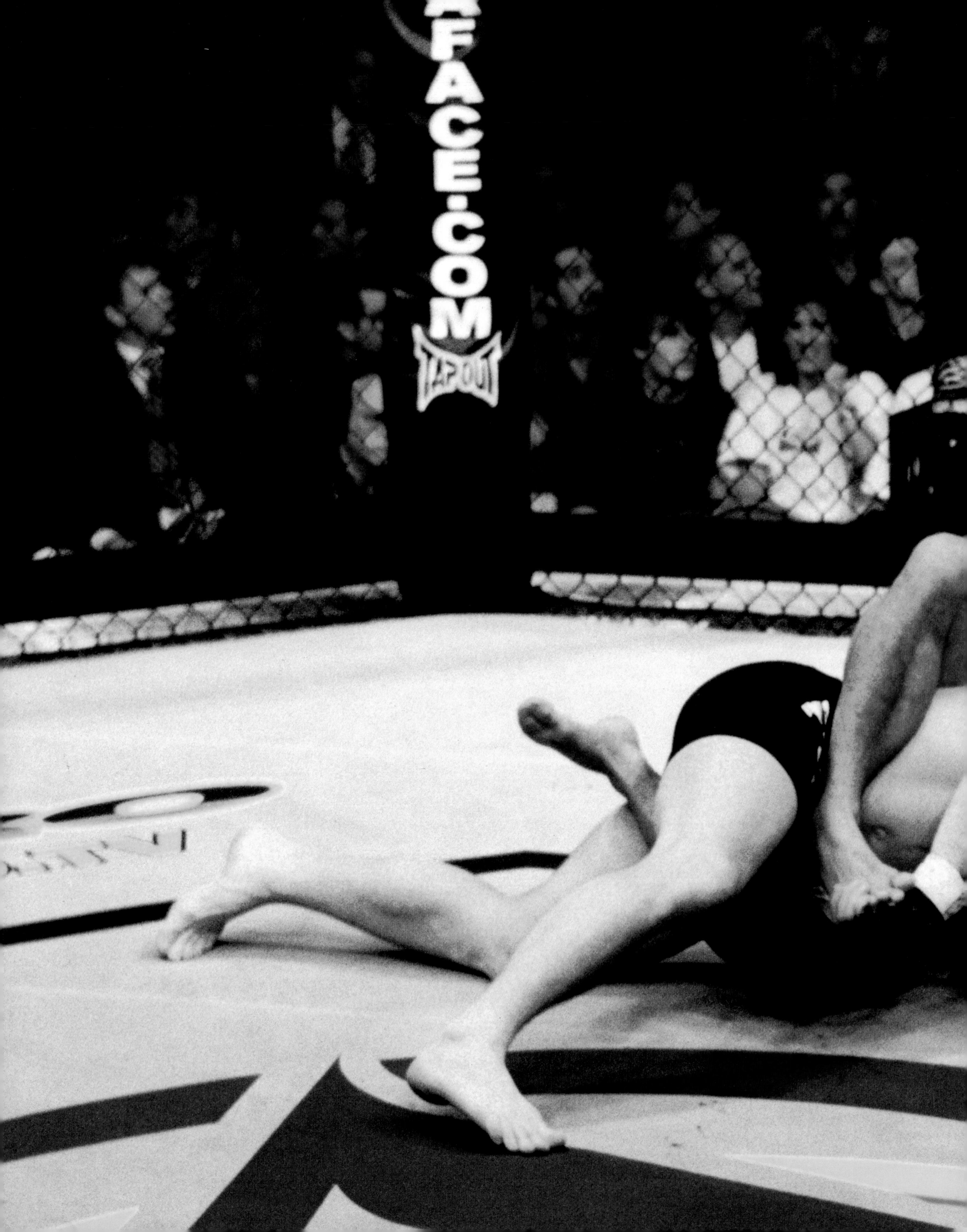
AFACE·COM
TAPOUT

The mental side is everything. The techniques have to be flawless, but the mind has to be tough. It has to be more flawless and you can never give up. I would even sit here and say that I'm in the entertainment business and the fight game business, but I'm also in the making you quit business. That's what it's all about.

B. J. PENN

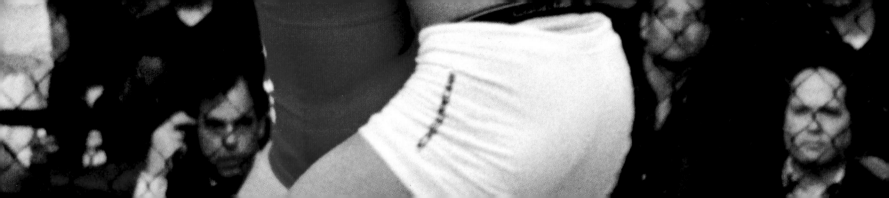

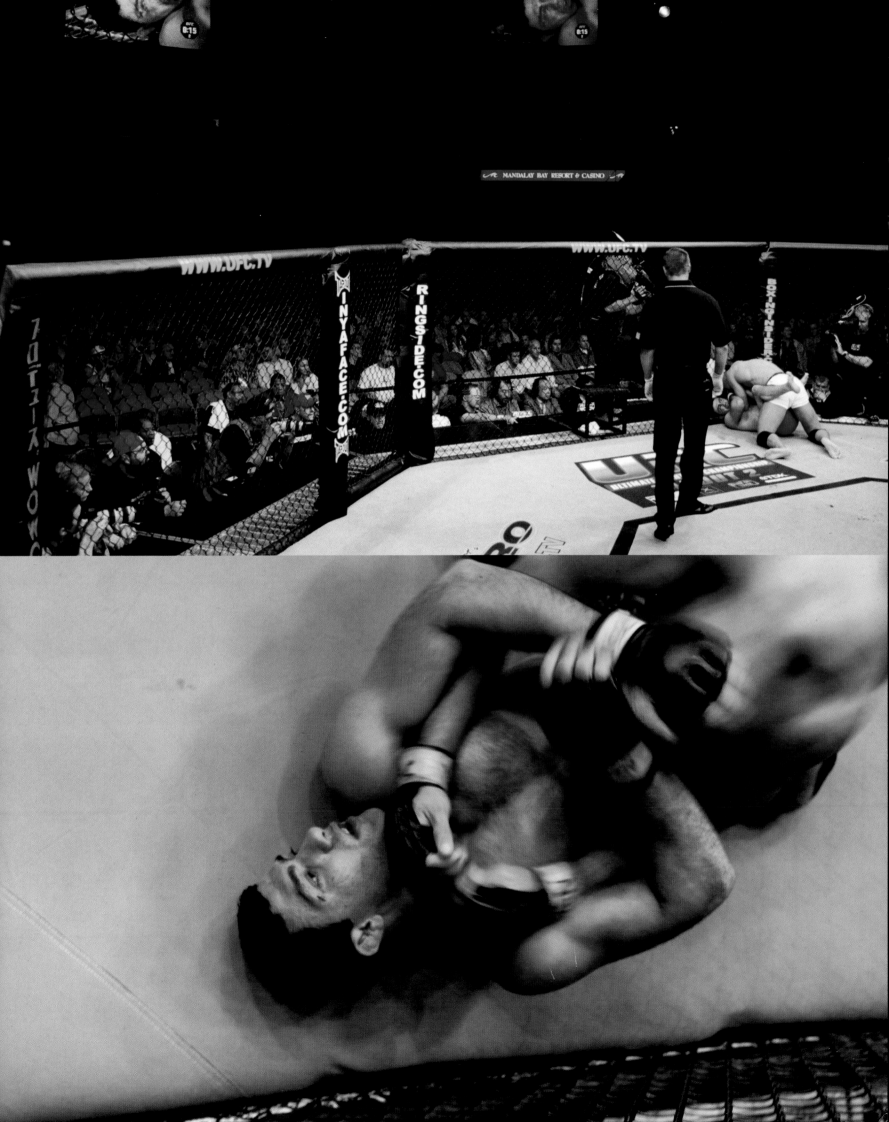

Quando você luta, você luta contra seus próprios erros. Você esta treinando e é bom ter desafios na vida—para escalar a montanha.

VITOR BELFORT

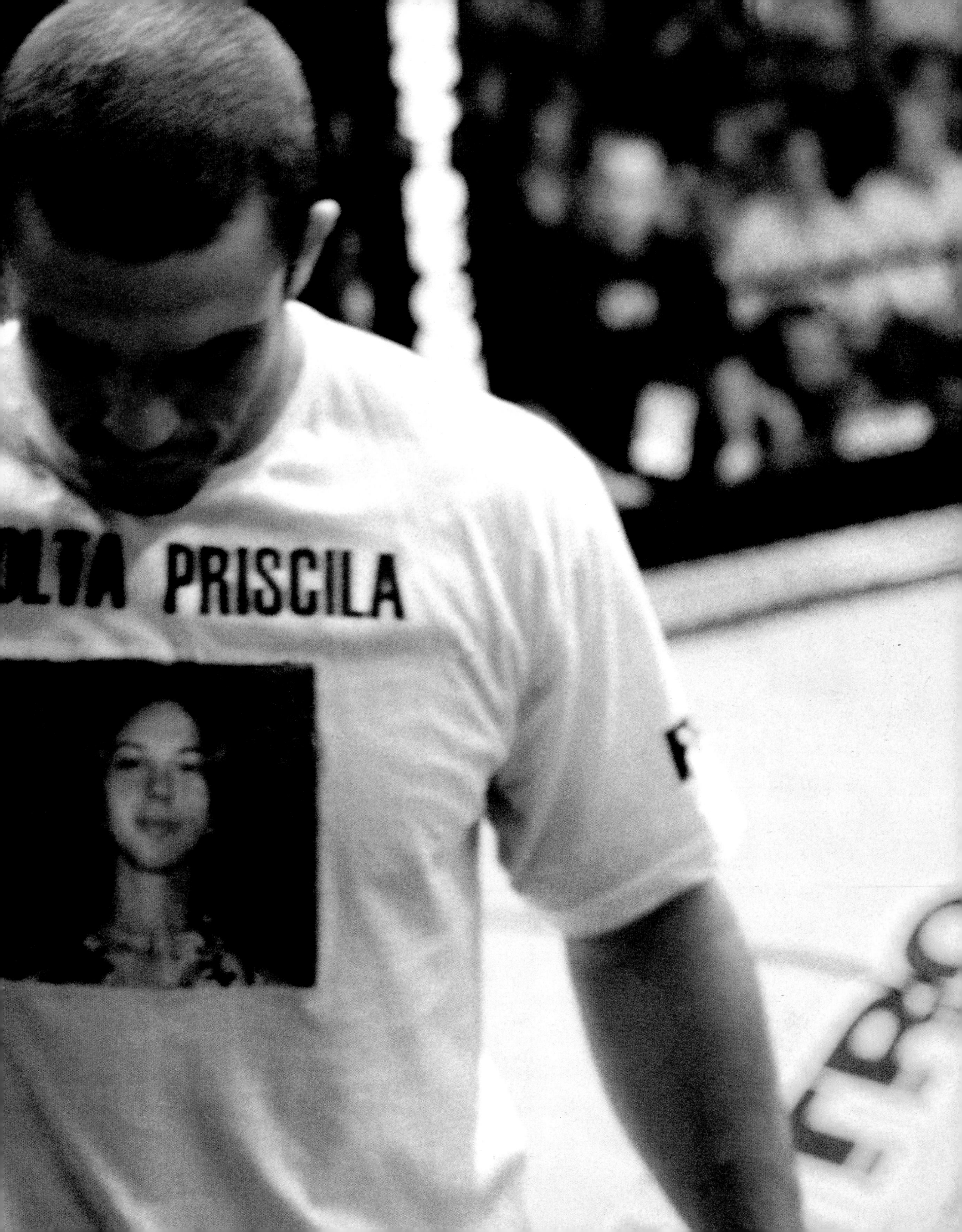
PRISCILA

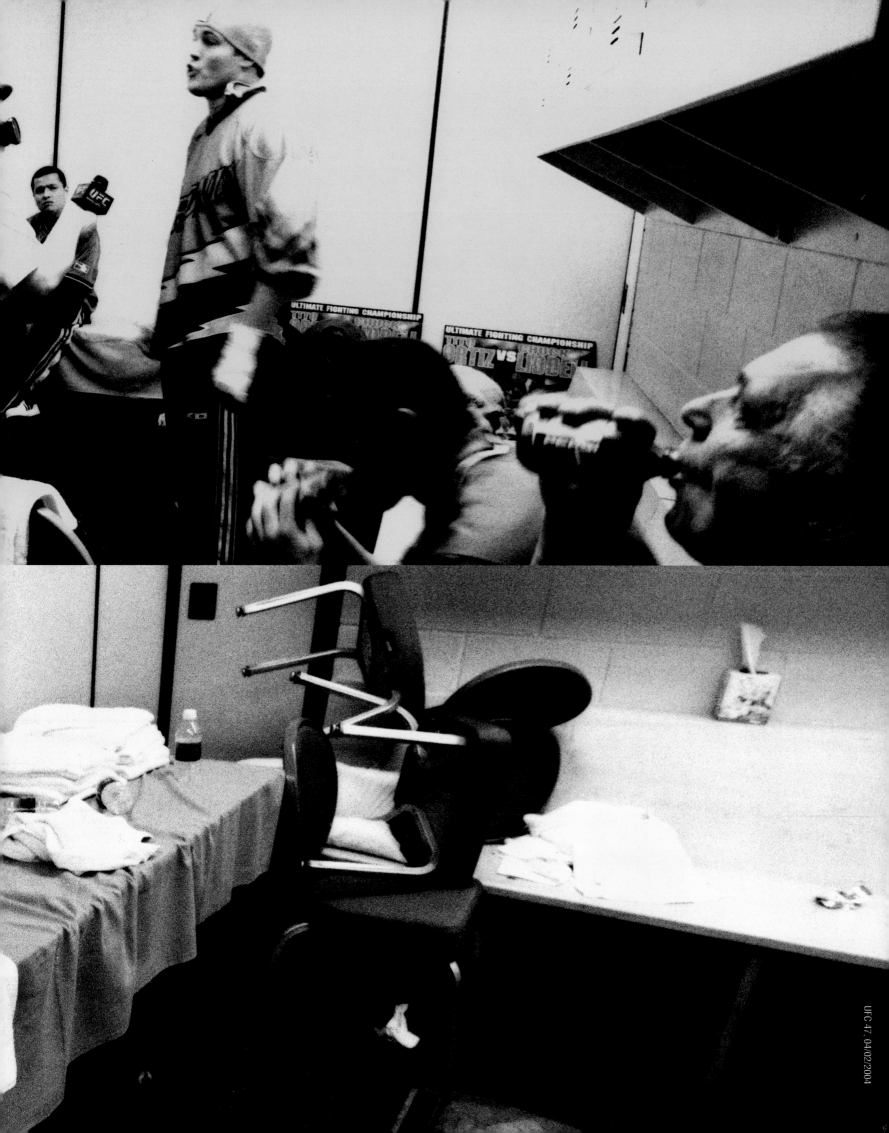

UFC 47, 04/02/2004

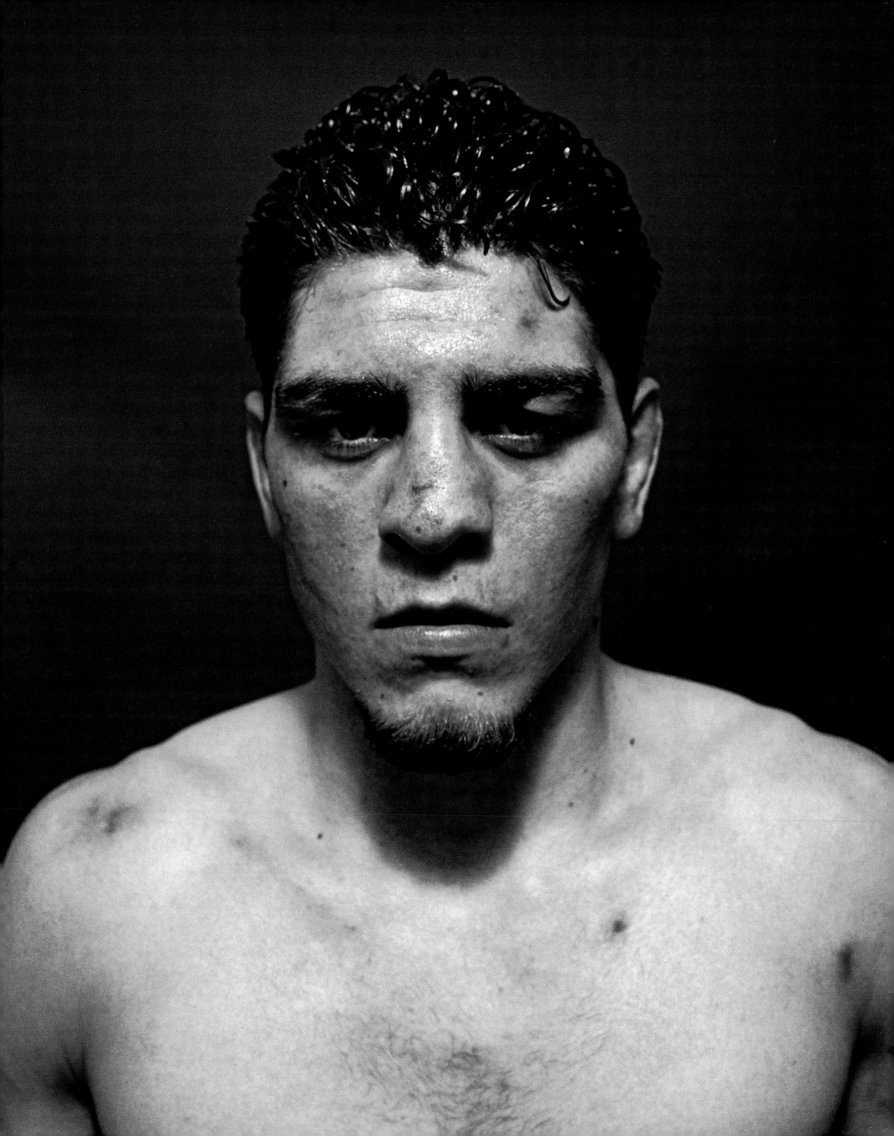

If I play baseball I'm going to hit home runs; if I'm playing defensive end I'm going to get sacks, and I'm going to make it look exciting. That's just the way I do stuff. It's not that I'm trying to do it. It's just natural. If the crowd likes it, they like it. If they don't, they don't, but usually they do.

ROBBIE LAWLER

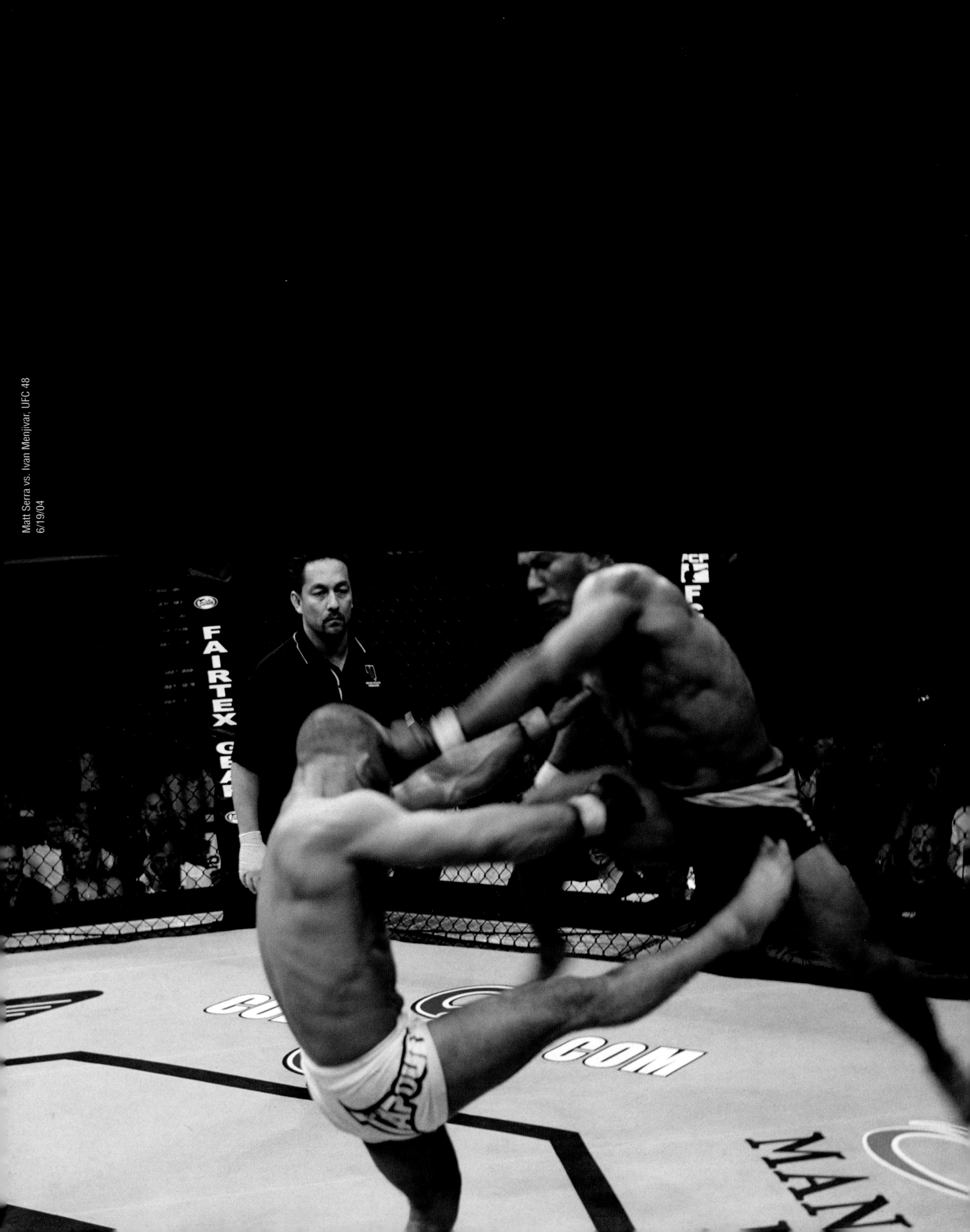

Matt Serra vs. Ivan Menjivar, UFC 48
6/19/04

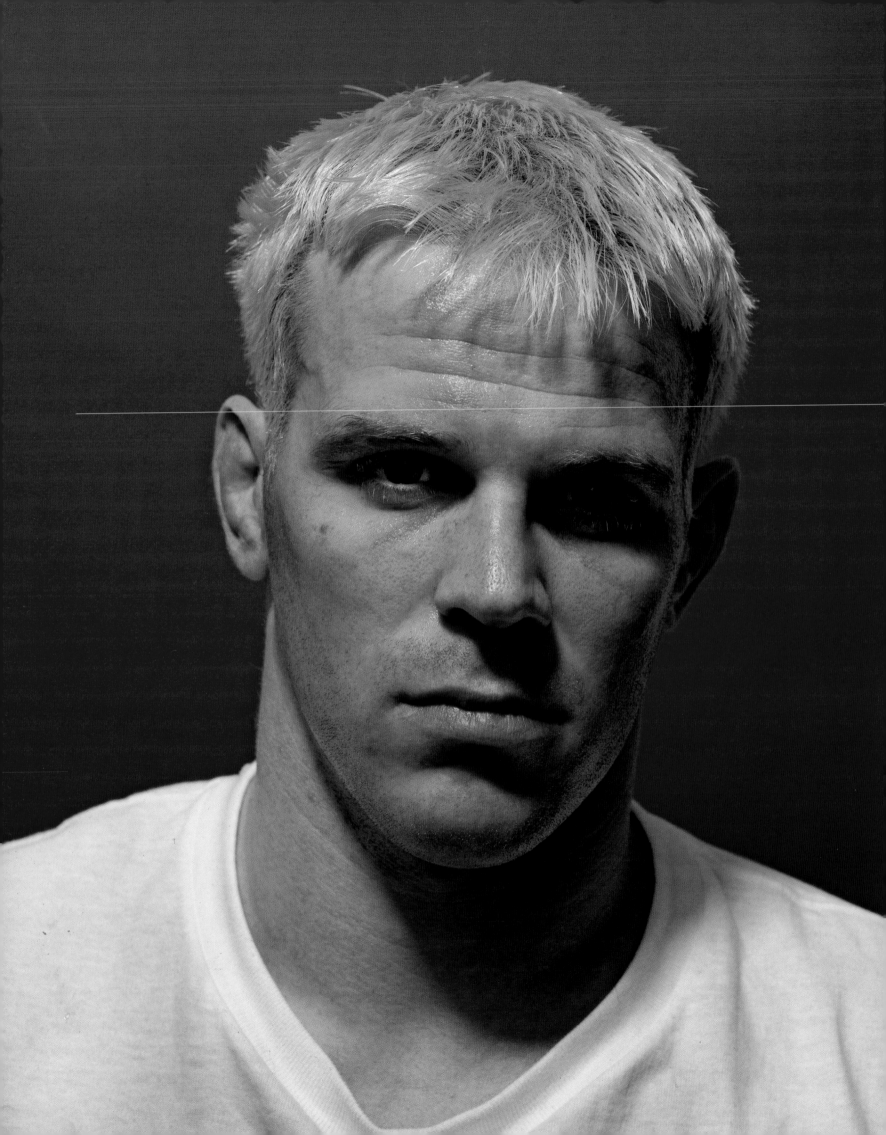

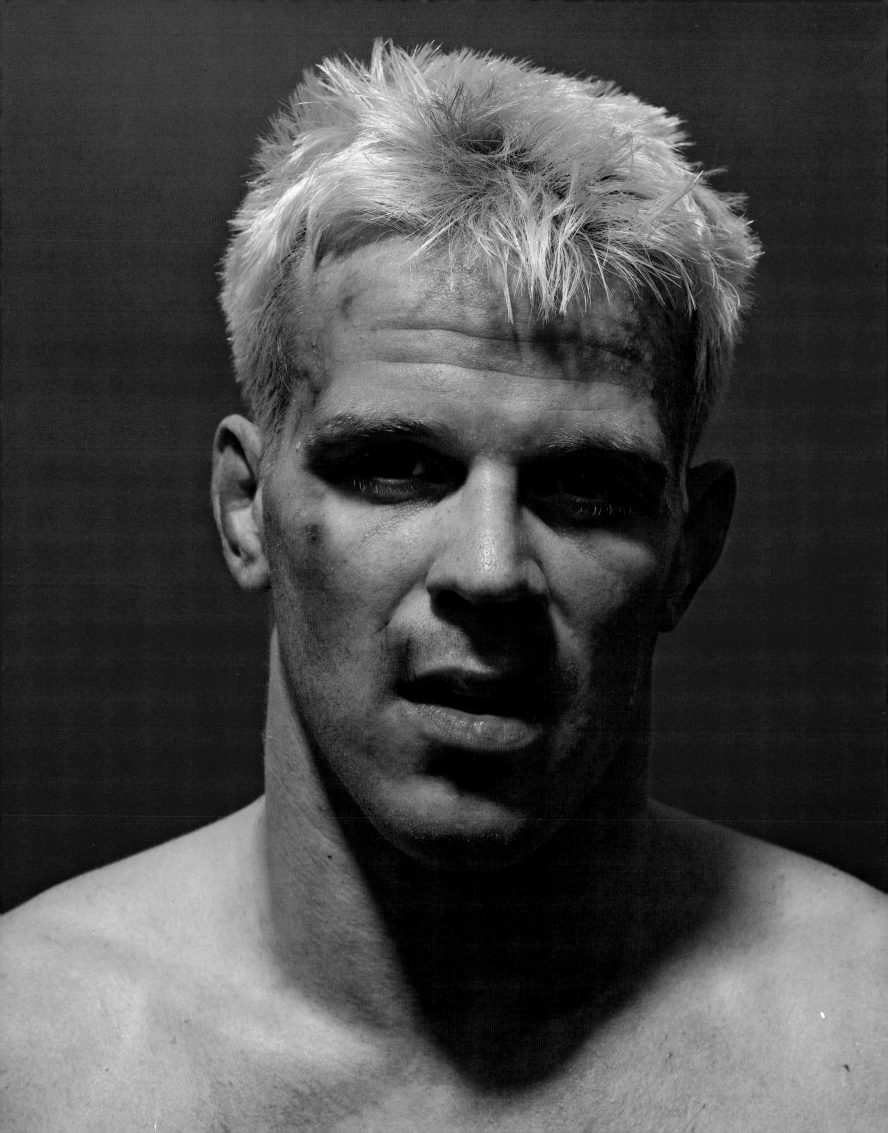

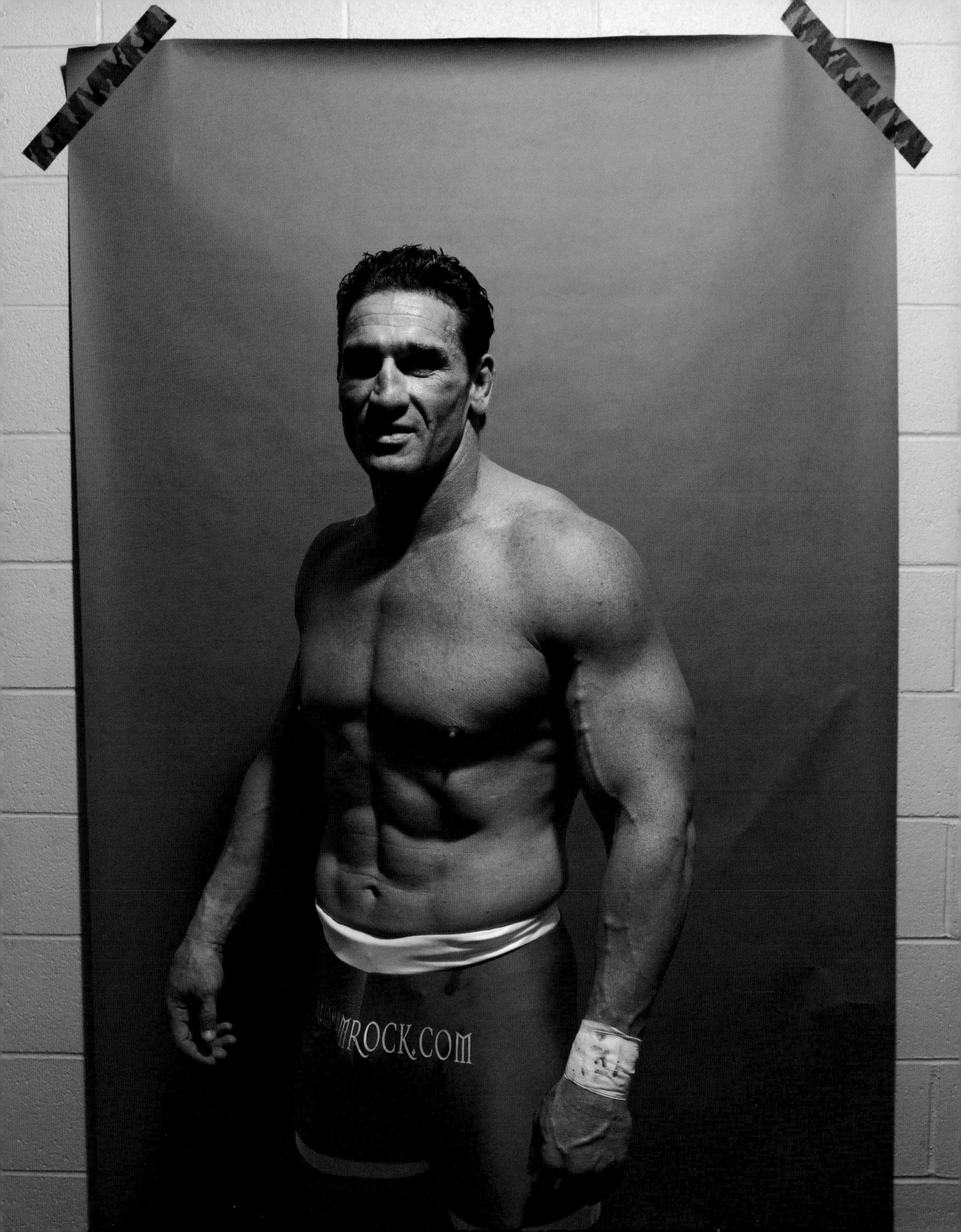
ROCK.COM

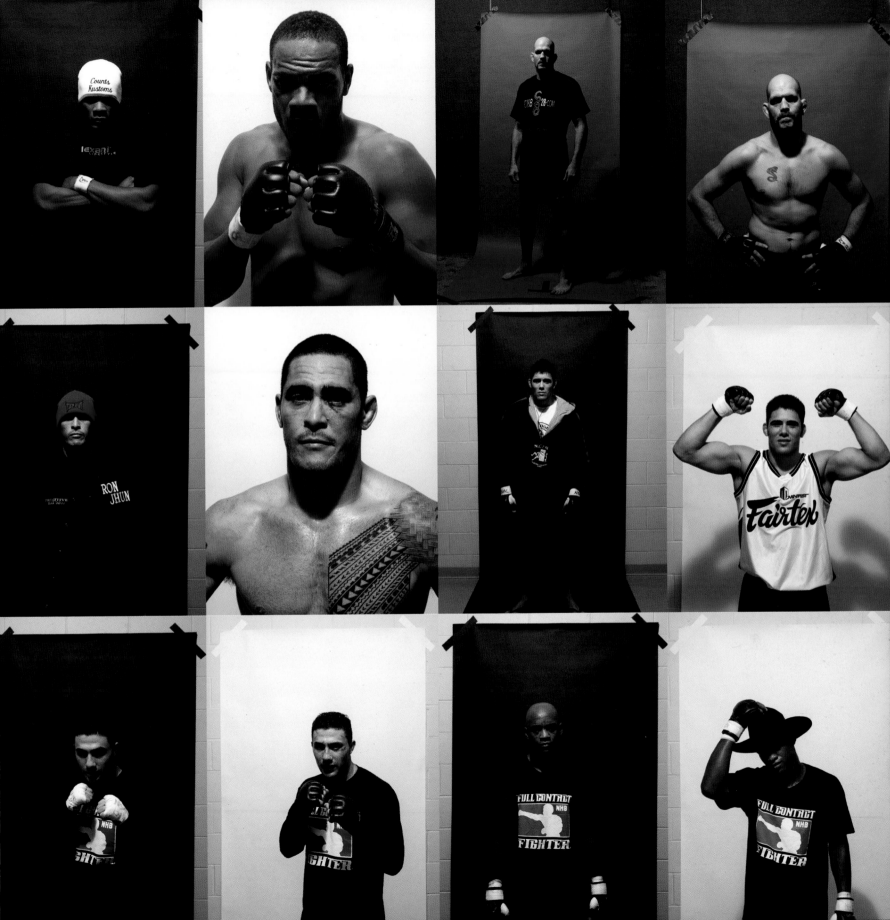

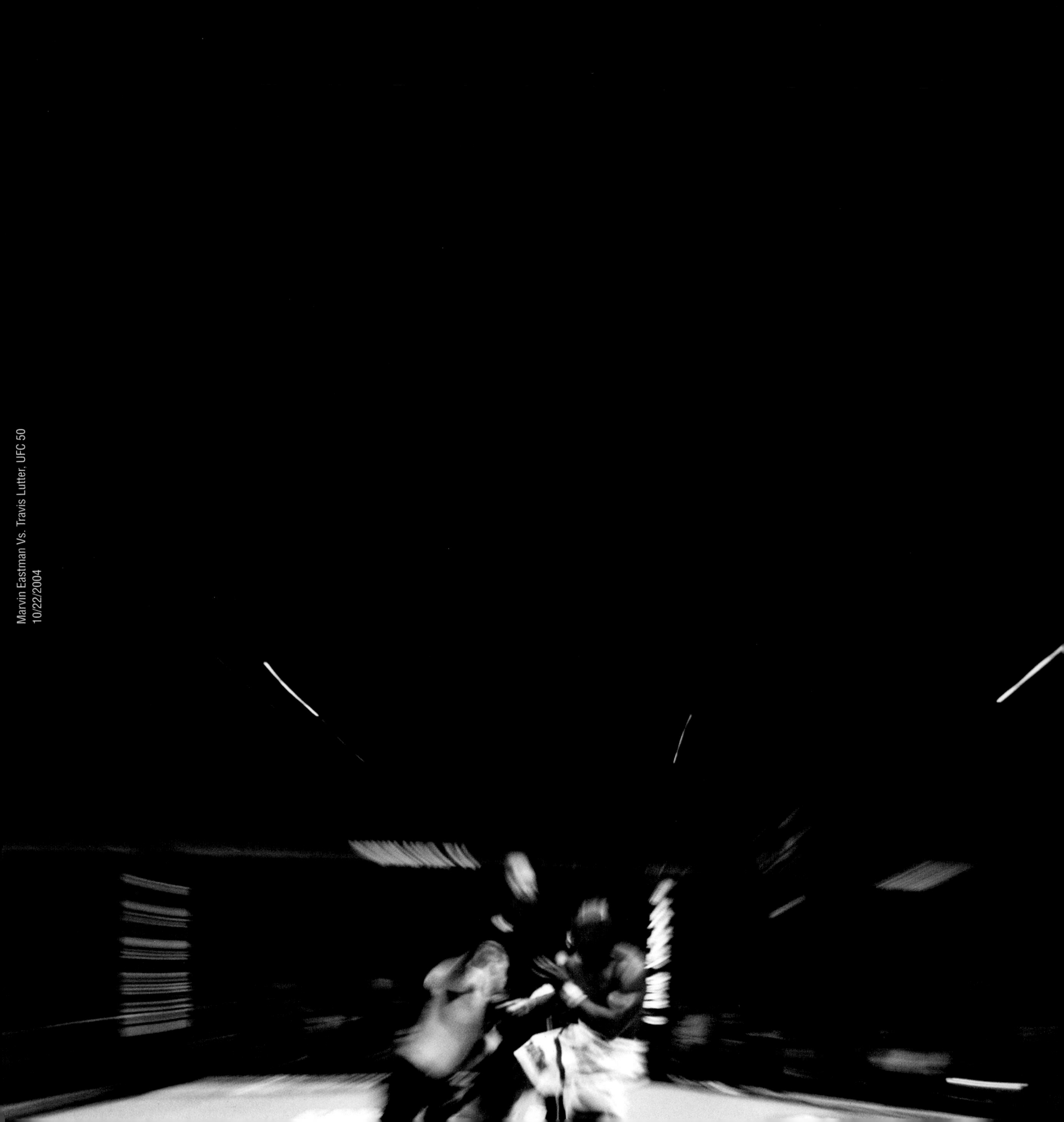

Marvin Eastman Vs. Travis Lutter, UFC 50
10/22/2004

KeN SHamRock's

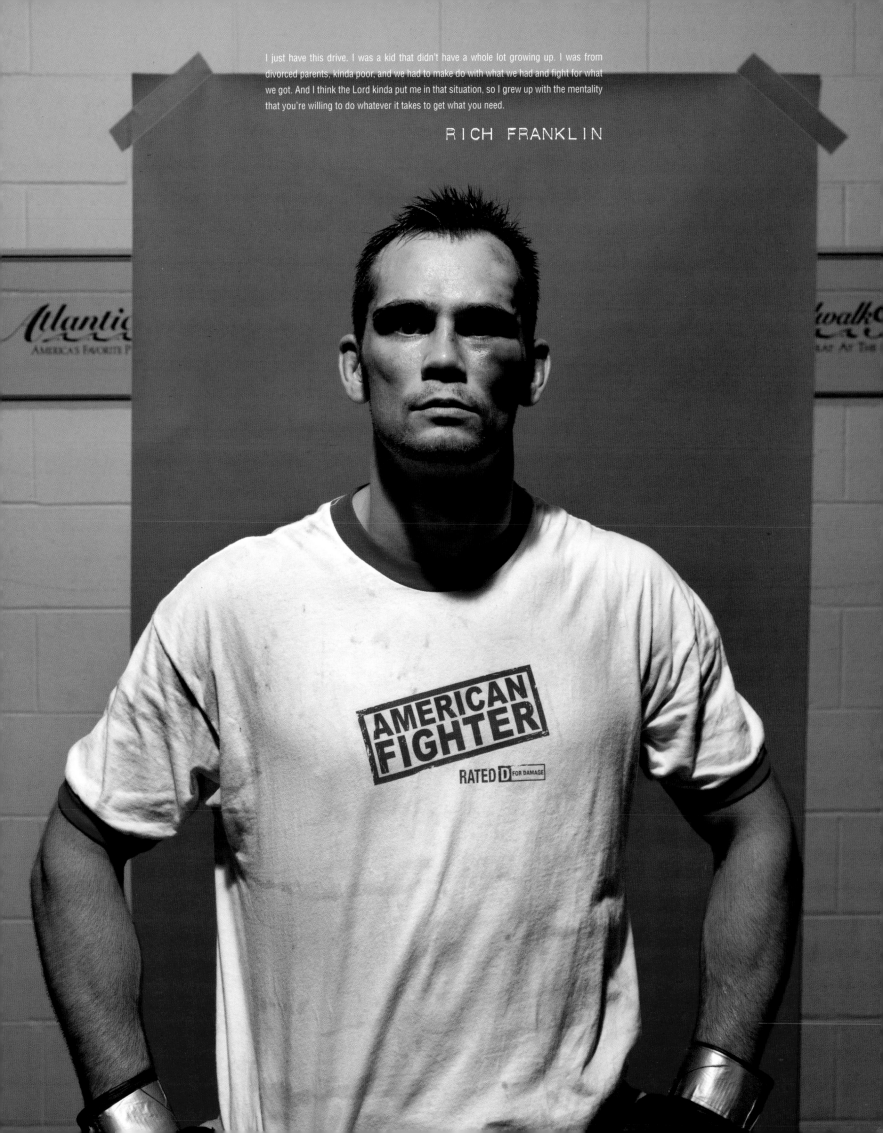

I just have this drive. I was a kid that didn't have a whole lot growing up. I was from divorced parents, kinda poor, and we had to make do with what we had and fight for what we got. And I think the Lord kinda put me in that situation, so I grew up with the mentality that you're willing to do whatever it takes to get what you need.

RICH FRANKLIN

Quand j'ai vu Royce Gracie participer au premier championnat de combat ultime, c'était comme le Super Bowl du combat libre (MMA). On peut être un champion de karaté, un champion de judo ou un champion de jiu-jitsu, mais quand on est le champion du combat ultime, on est le champion de toutes les disciplines.

GEORGES ST-PIERRE

FULL CONTACT

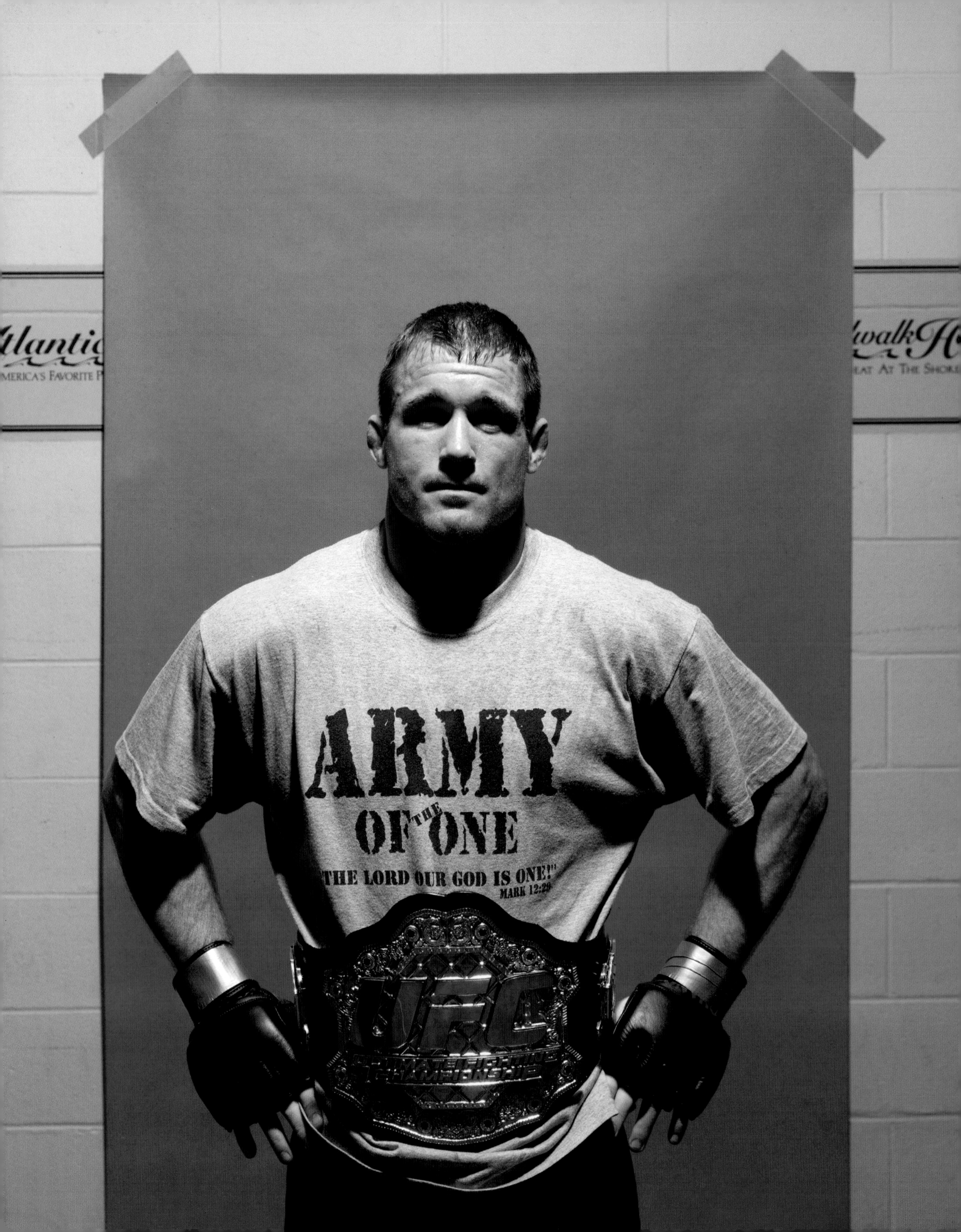
ARMY
OF THE ONE
"THE LORD OUR GOD IS ONE!"
MARK 12:29
UFC

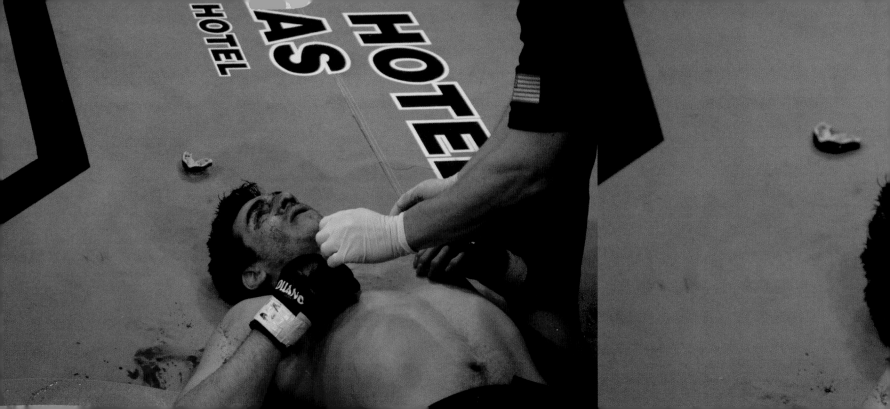

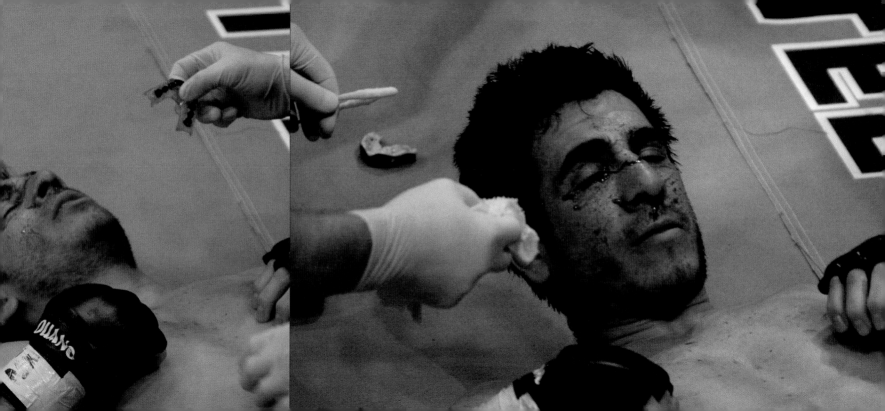

You learn in economics about competition over limited resources. I'm pretty self-centered and I want what's best for me. I need to win this fight, just like he does, and I understand that he's going to do everything in his power to win it, and I certainly don't resent that or hold it against him at all. I'm gonna do the same thing.

FORREST GRIFFIN

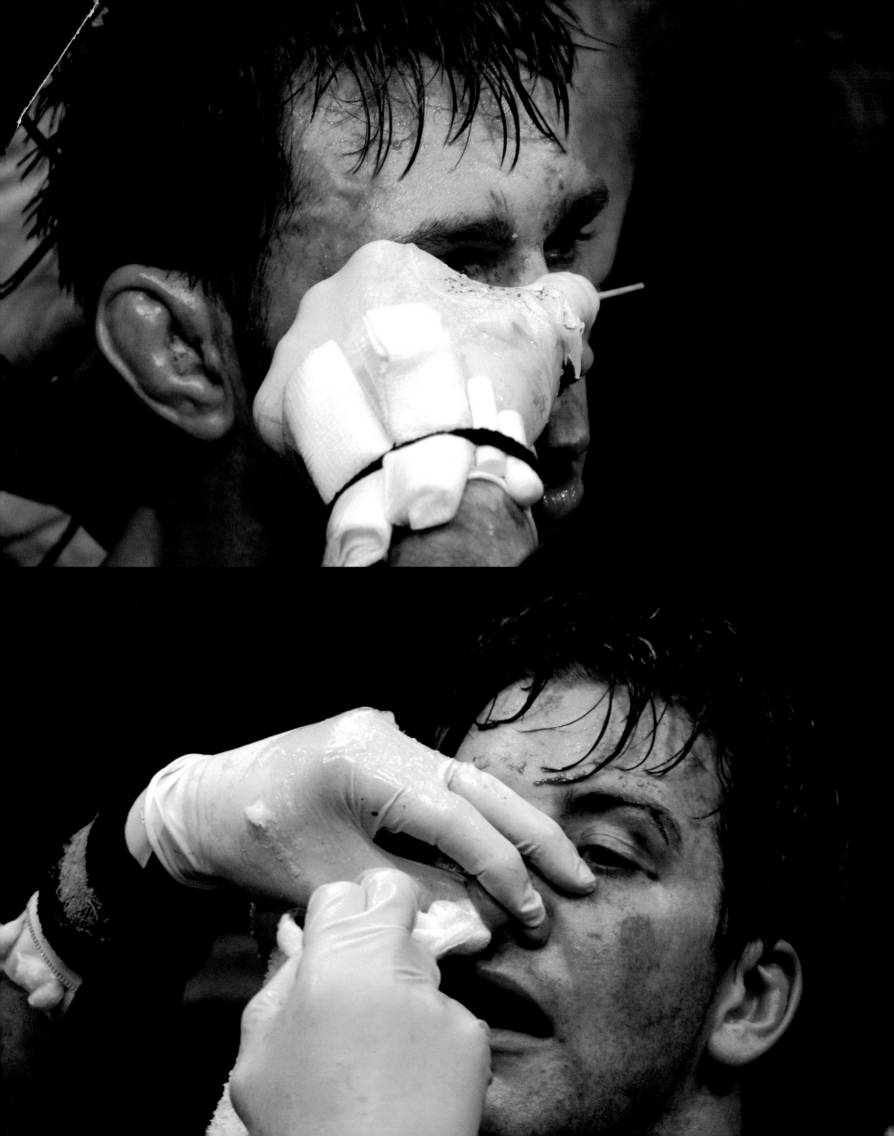

WWW.UFC.TV
FCFIGHTER.COM

MGM GRAND
WWW.UFC.TV
XYIENCE.COM
FAIRTEX GEAR
TEAM
WHERE THE
FIGHT BEGINS
.COM
28.COM

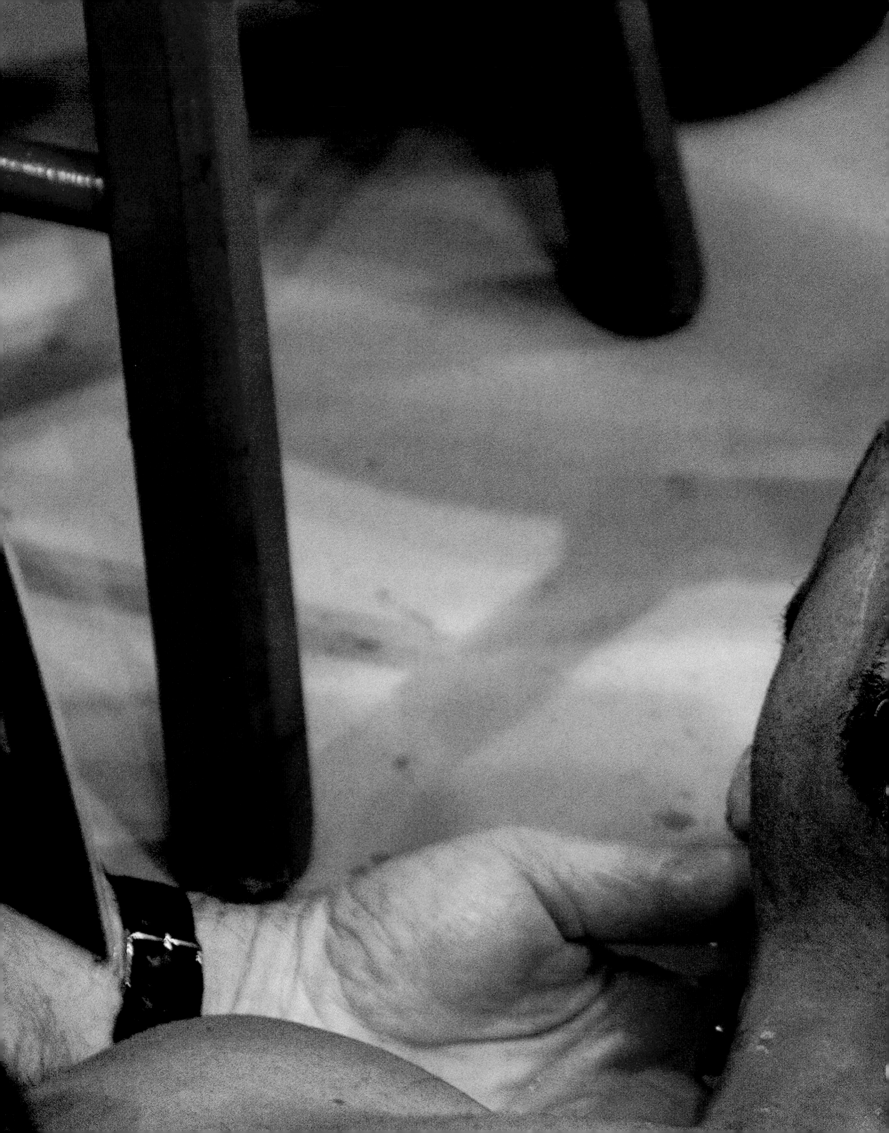

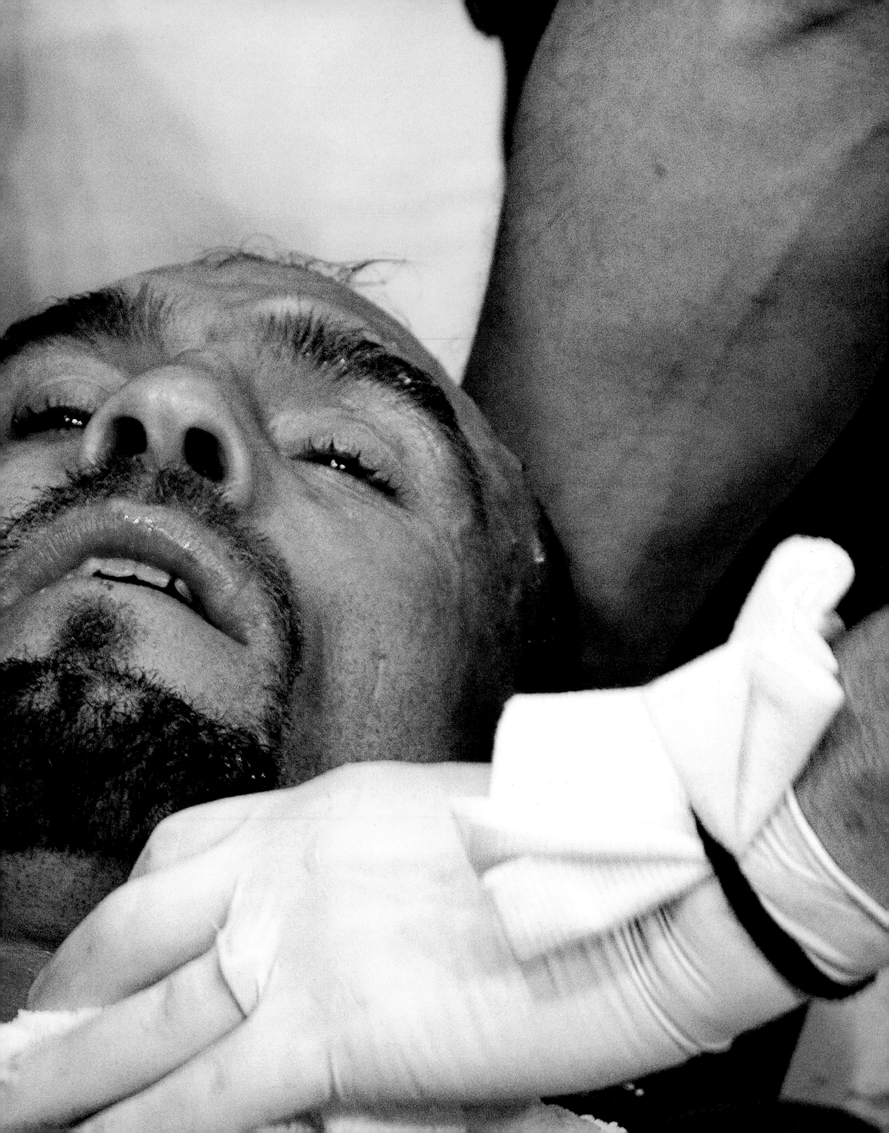

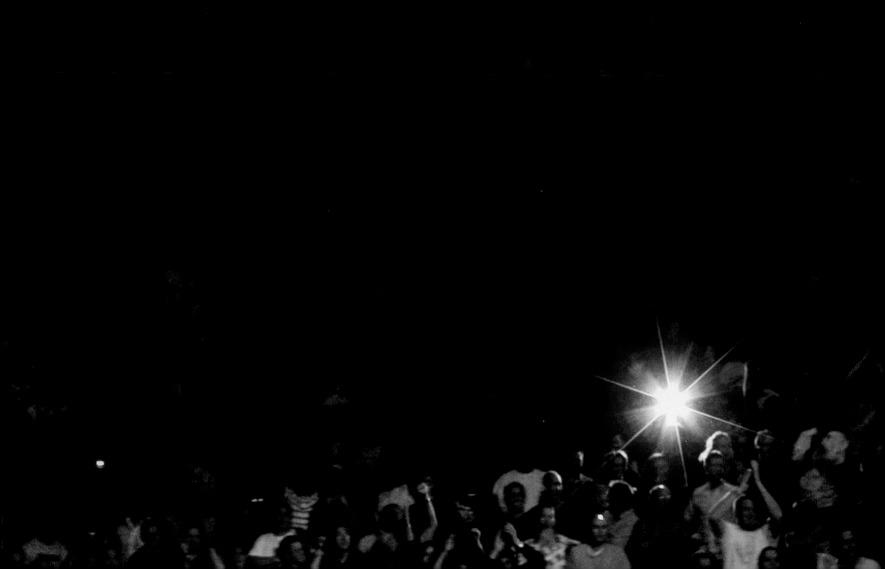

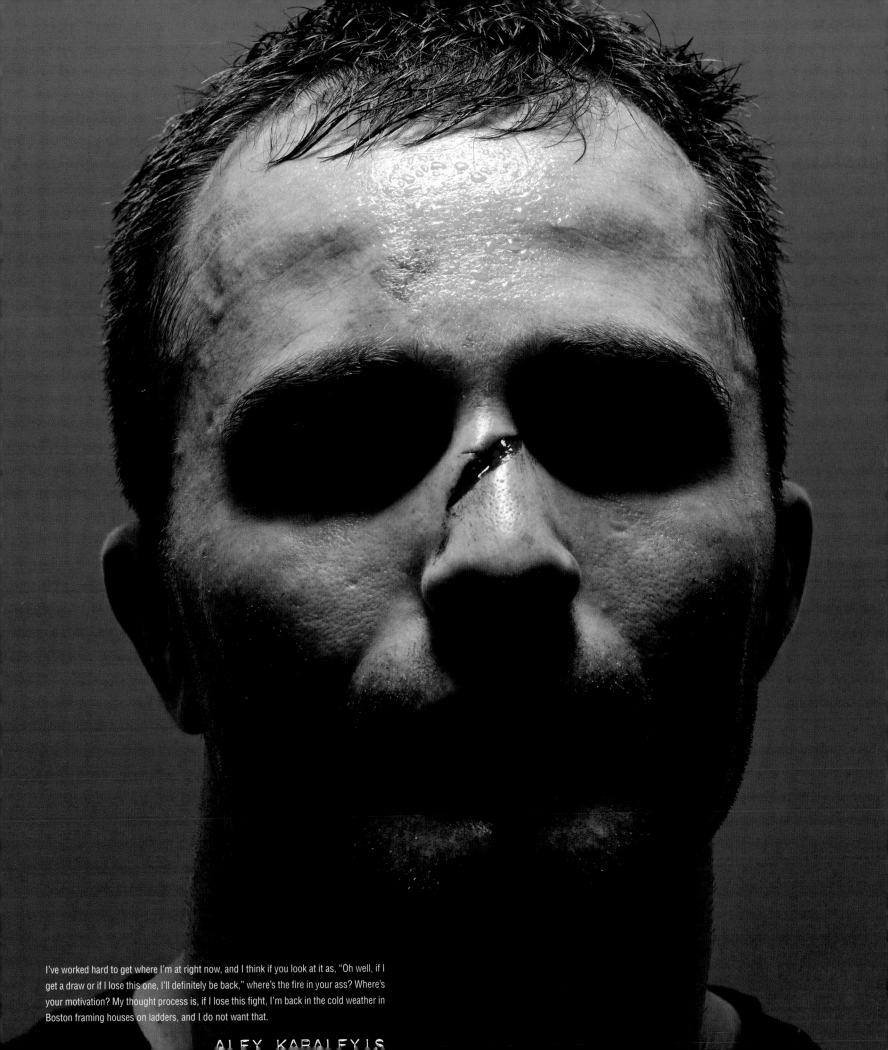

I've worked hard to get where I'm at right now, and I think if you look at it as, "Oh well, if I get a draw or if I lose this one, I'll definitely be back," where's the fire in your ass? Where's your motivation? My thought process is, if I lose this fight, I'm back in the cold weather in Boston framing houses on ladders, and I do not want that.

ALEX KARALEXIS

Questo è qualcosa che ho realmente dentro di me. Si tratta di uno sport che mi consente di sfidare me stesso e di seguire la strada dell'onore e lo spirito combattente. Il mio destino era di diventare un pugile e perciò sono felice di trovarmi ora in un posto che sembra fatto per me.

ALESSIO SAKARA

I'm a professional at my job; fighting is what I do. It's not a street fight. It's not a personal confrontation. It's business when I go in there.

DIEGO SANCHEZ

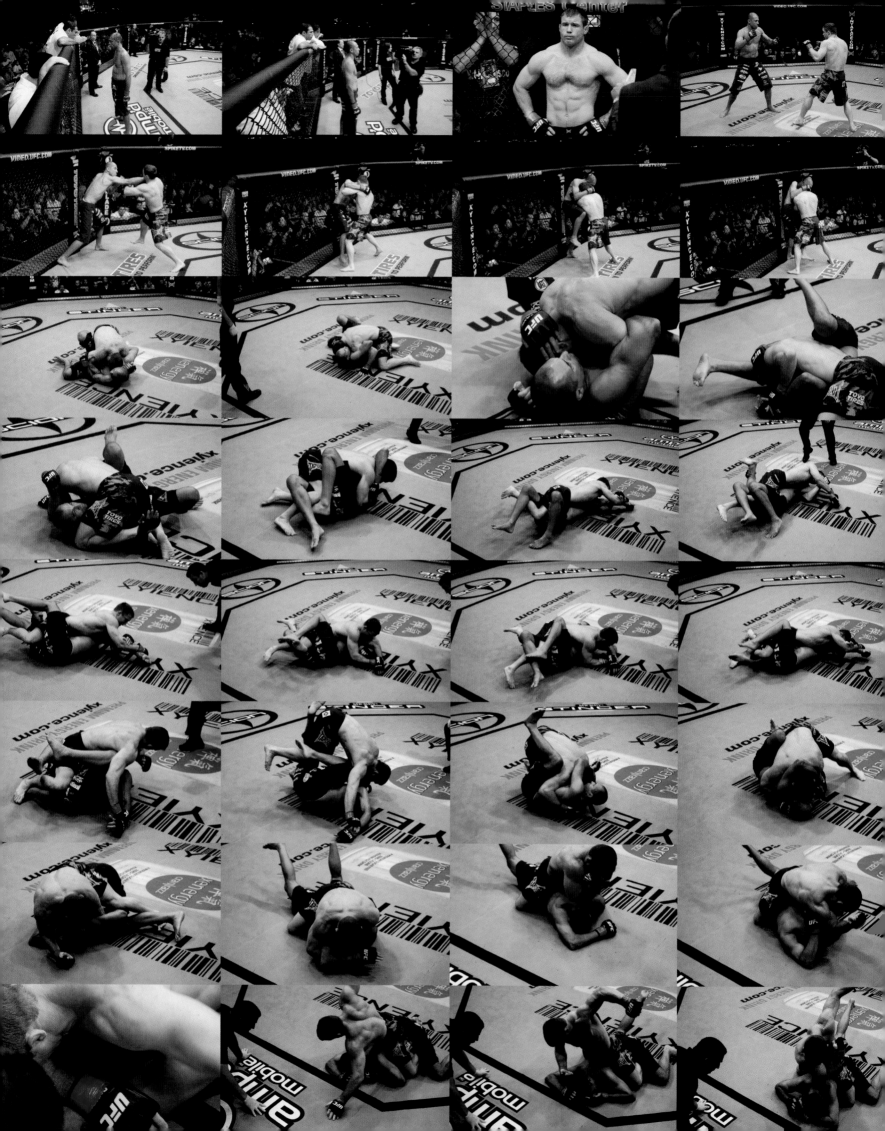

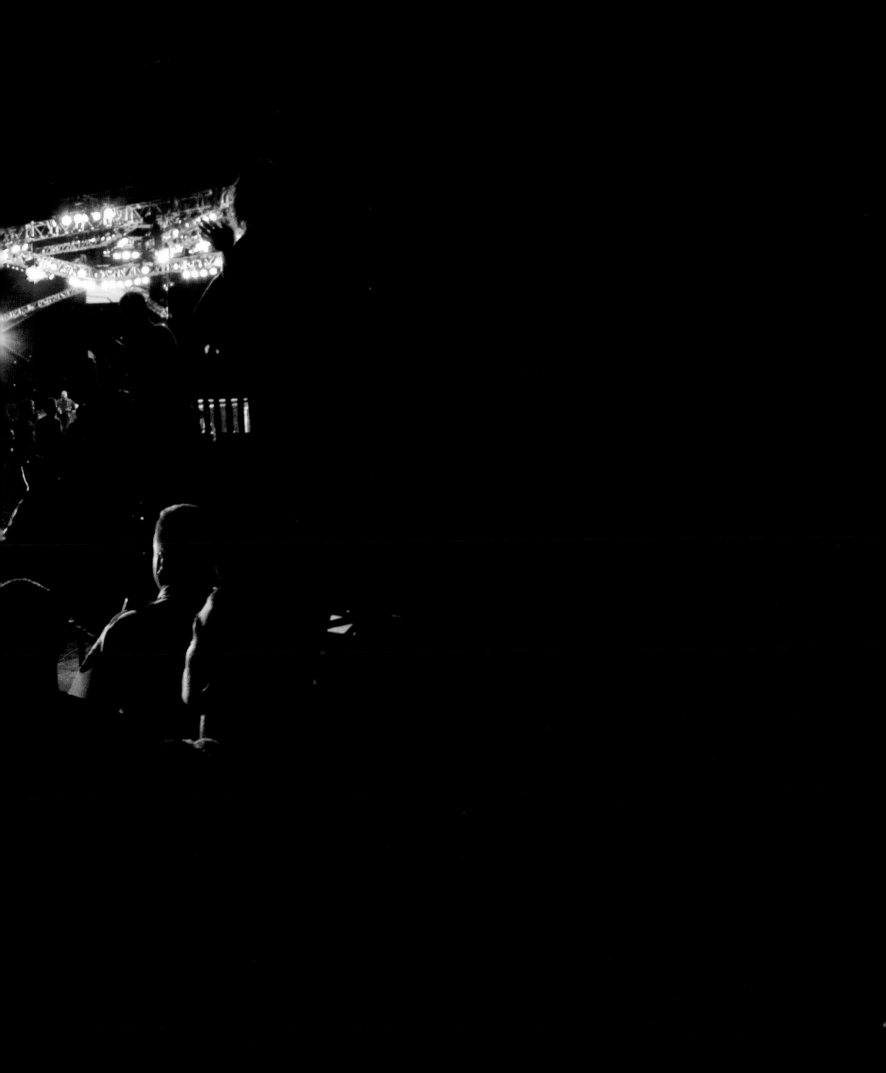

Практически, каждый, кто вступает в Октагон как претендент (соперник), является угрозой. Я воспринимаю всех моих оппонентов (противников) серьёзно, я уважаю их всех и я понимаю, что они не попадают туда случайно либо по совпадению. Существуют причины, по которым люди получают возможность бороться за звание (титул)

ANDREI ARLOVSKI

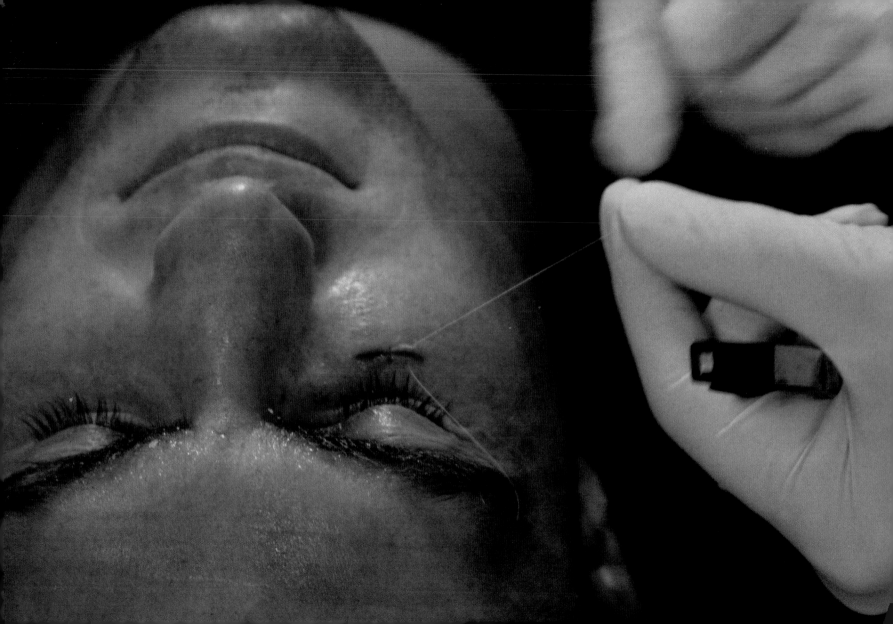

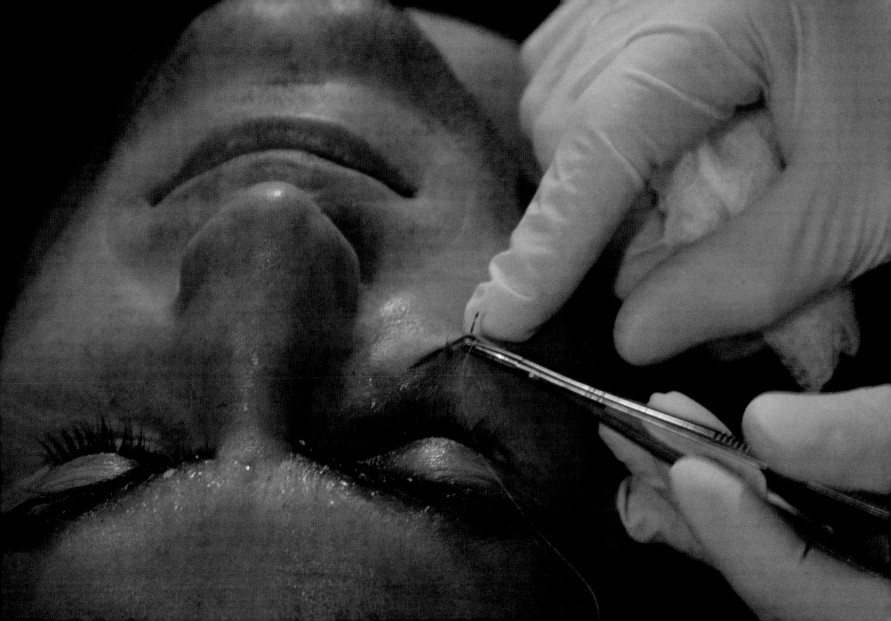

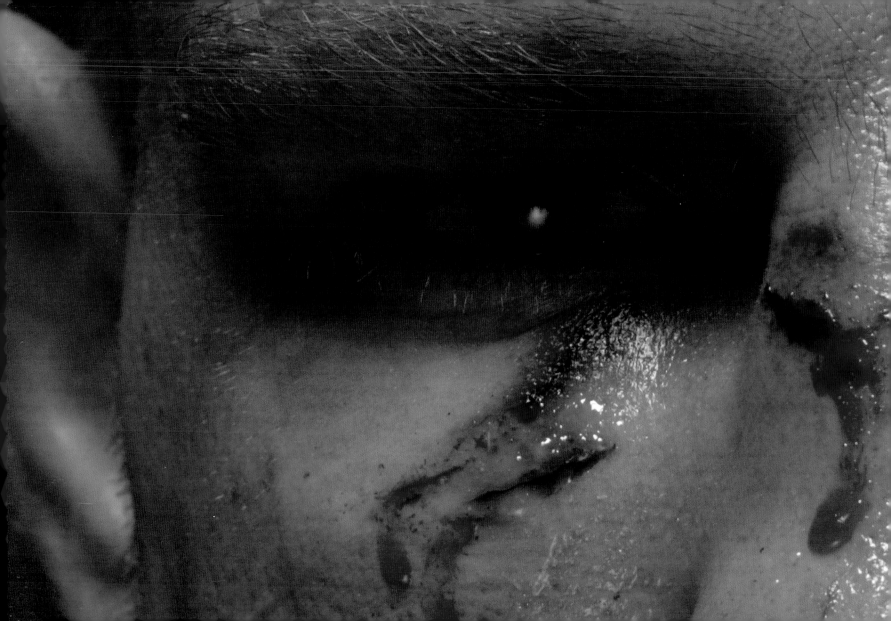

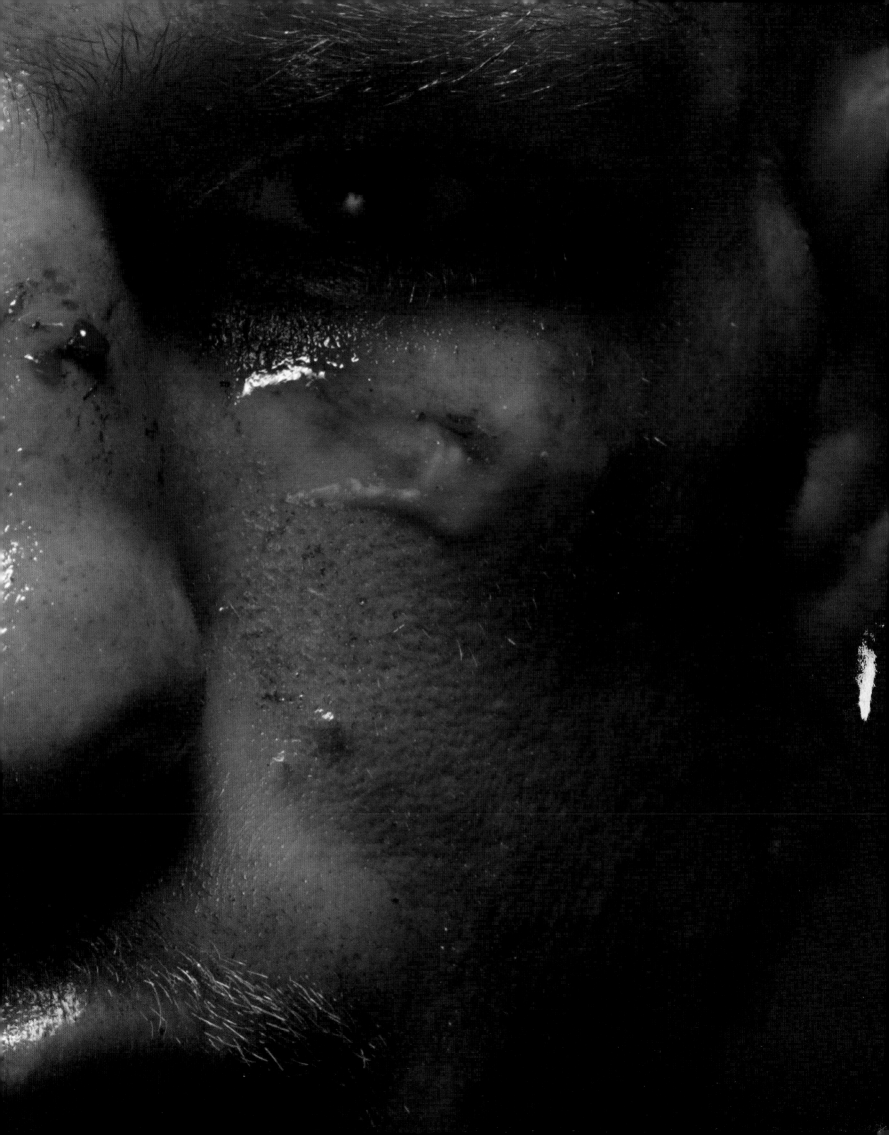

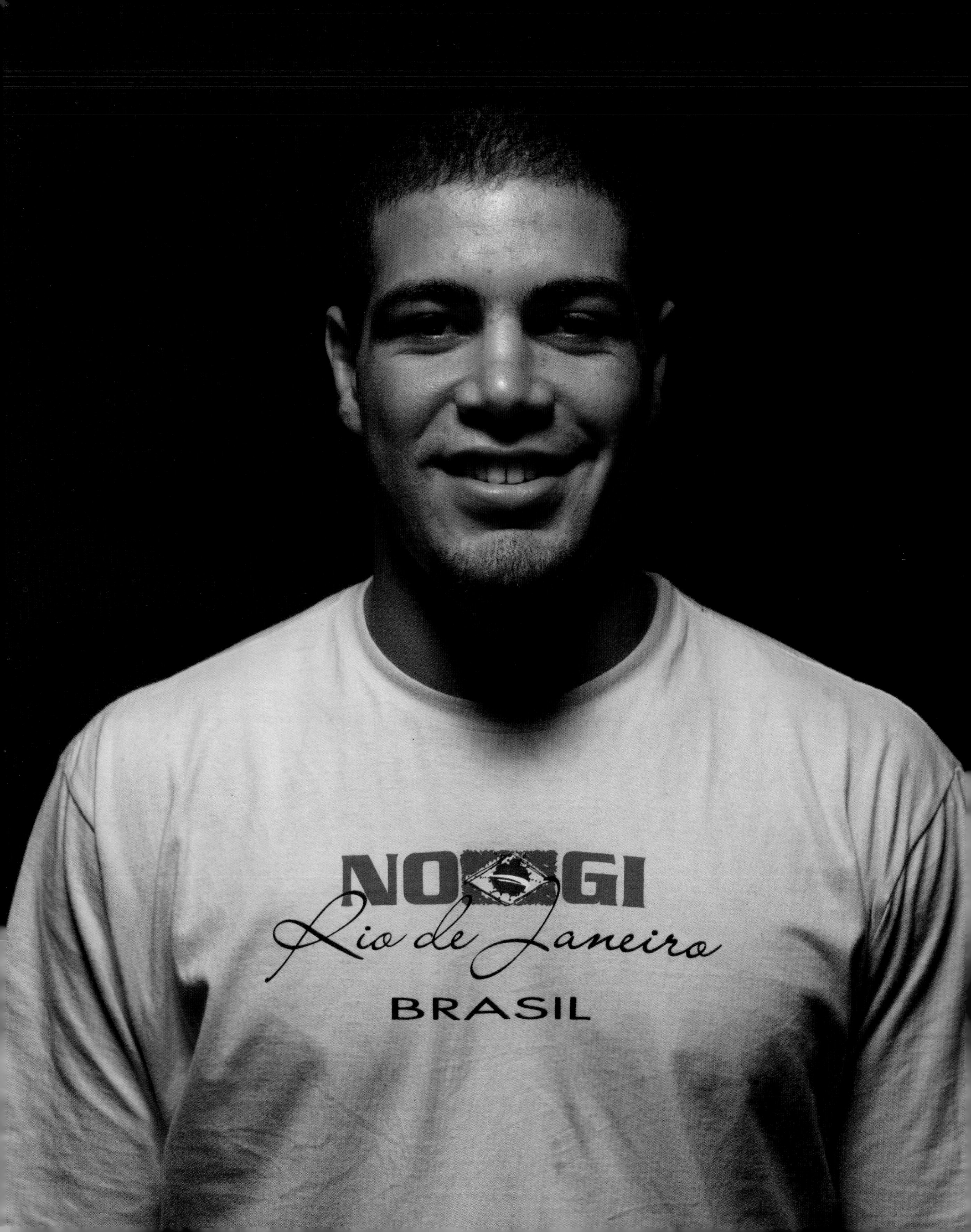
NO GI
Rio de Janeiro
BRASIL

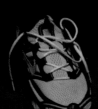

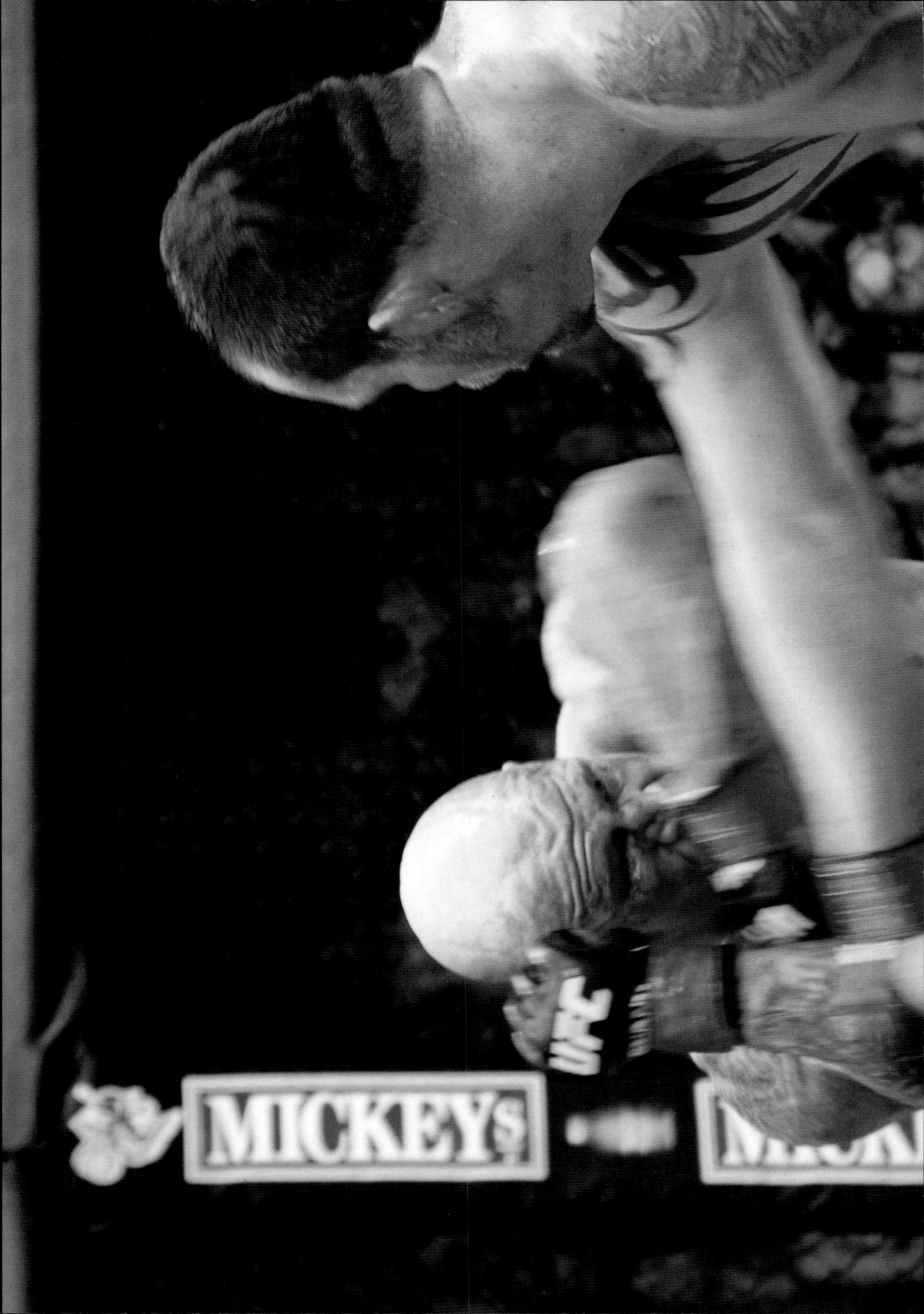

Tim Sylvia Vs. Jeff Monson, UFC 65
11/18/2006

Ես մի տղա էի, որը կռվում էր 20-ից բարձր տղաների հետ, 230 ֆունտ միայն մկան, և ես կոտրում էի նրանց քթերը և խեղդում նրանց առաջին ռաունդում: Այդ ժամանակ դրա մասին շատ չէի մտածում: Ես դեռ դպրոց էի գնում: Երբ ես 16 էի, ես կռվեցի Գրեյսի վարդապետուն գոտիի հետ: Նա եկավ իր երեխաների հետ: Նա 34 տարեկան էր: Չեմ ուզում անարգել նրան, բայց դա նույնիսկ կռիվ էլ չէր: Ես խաղում էի նրա հետ: Նա հագել էր ծլուտո ջի, այնպես որ ես ընդամենը բռնում էի նրան և նետում: Վերջապես, ես գետնեցի նրան և սկսեցի ուղղակի խեղդում հետունից, և հաջորդ օրը գնացի դպրոց:

KARO PARISYAN

UFC Fight Night 7, Marine Corps Air Station Miramar
12/13/2006

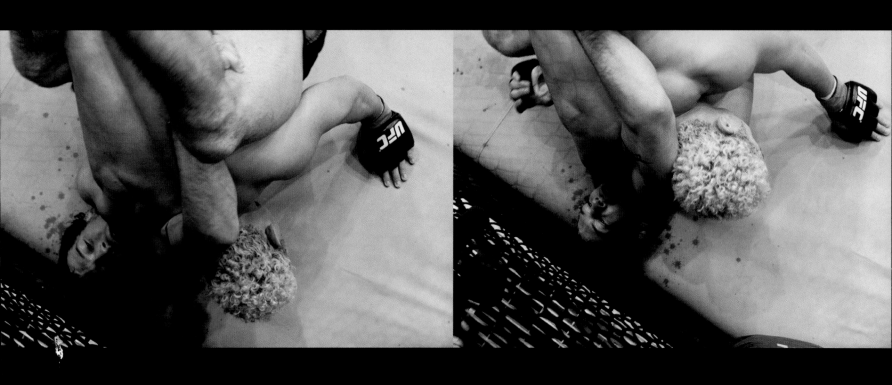

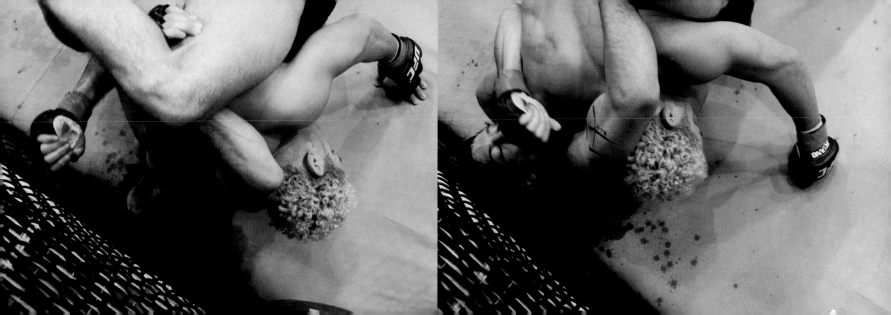

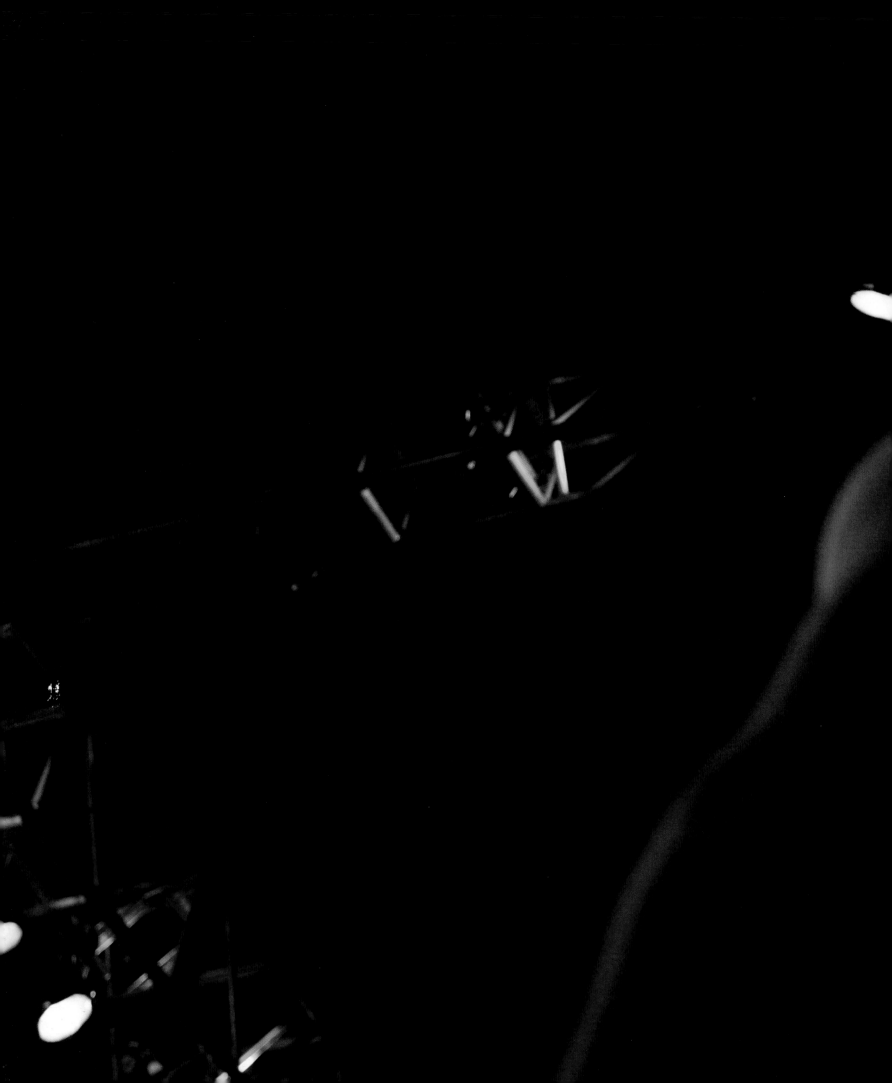

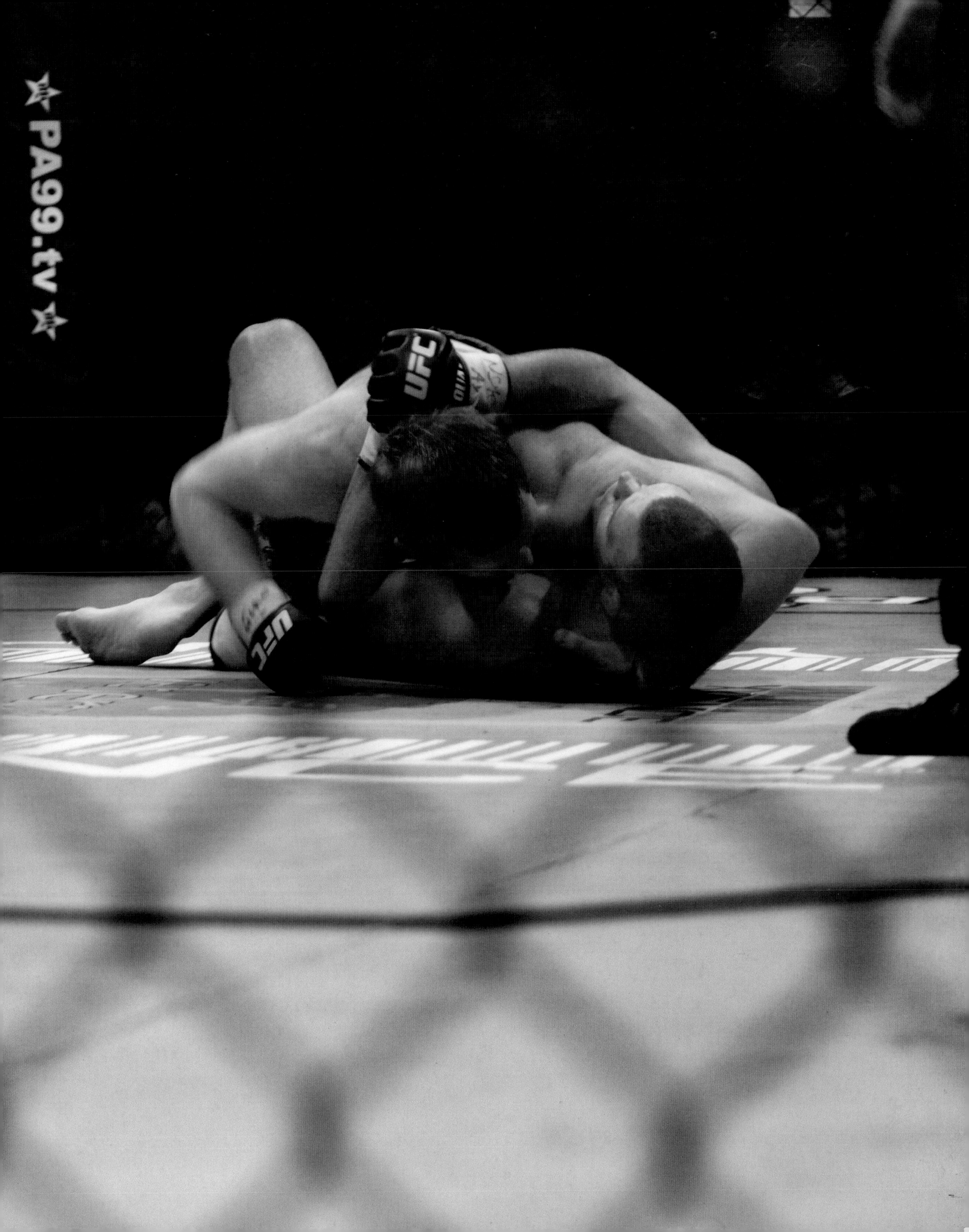
PA99.tv
UFC
UFC

AMOR

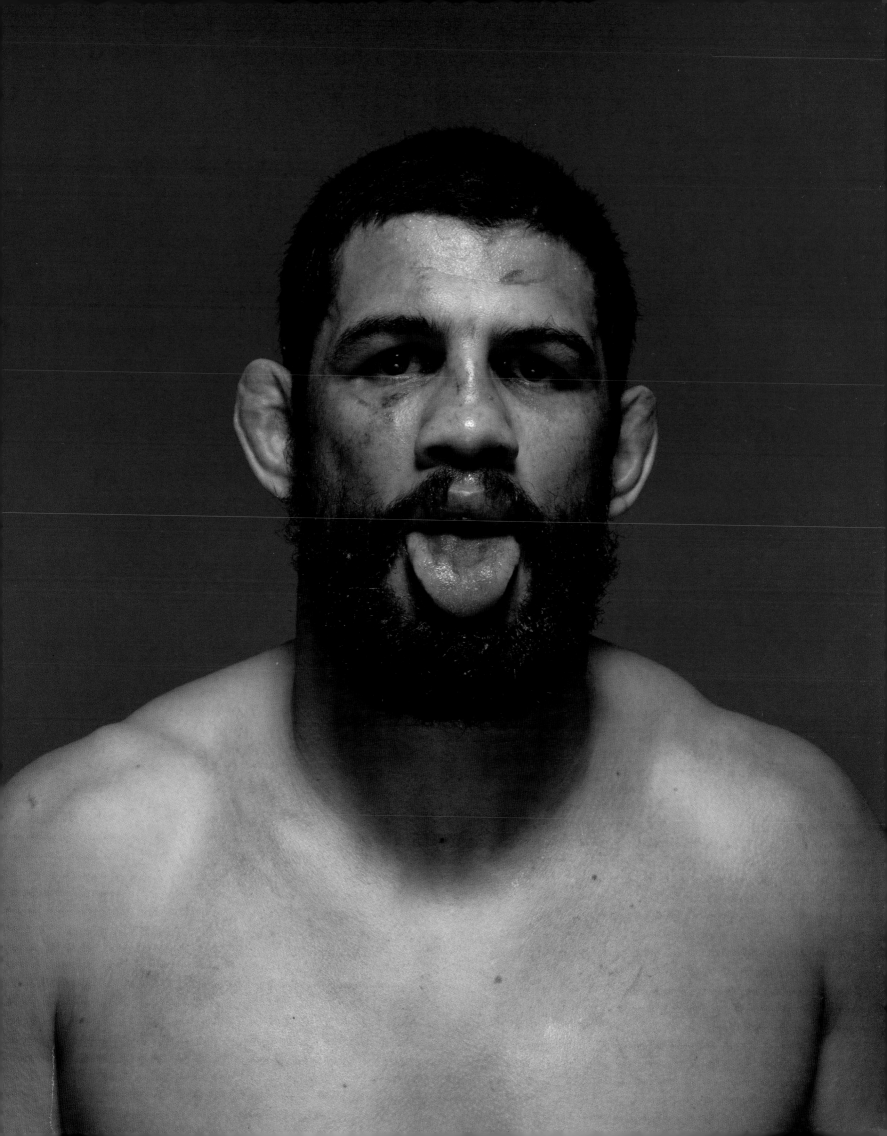

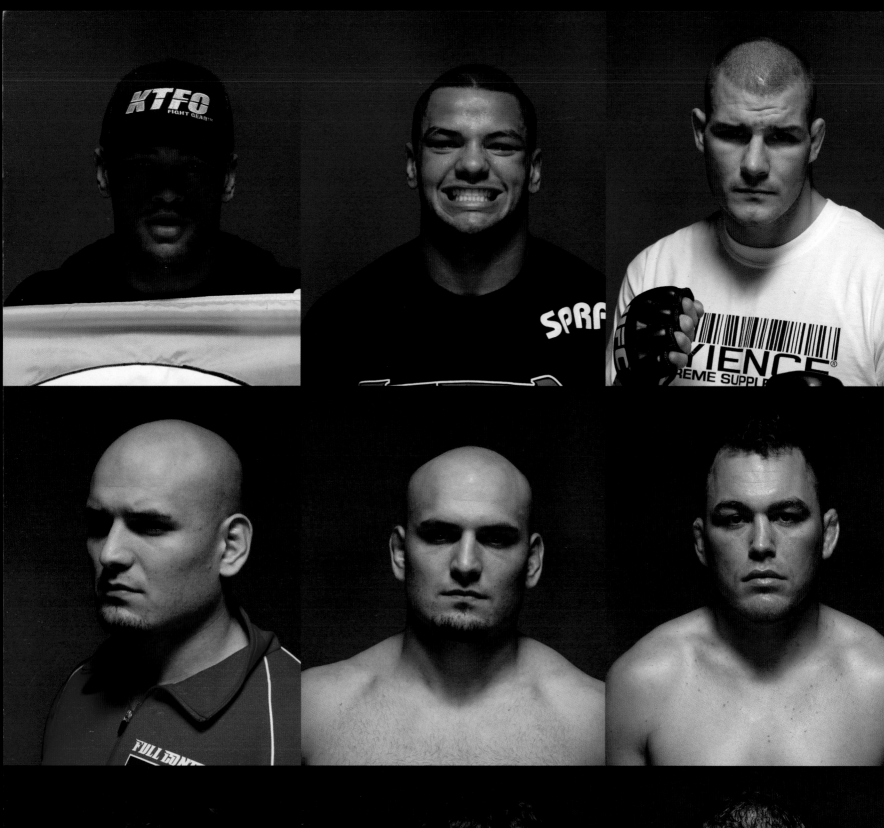

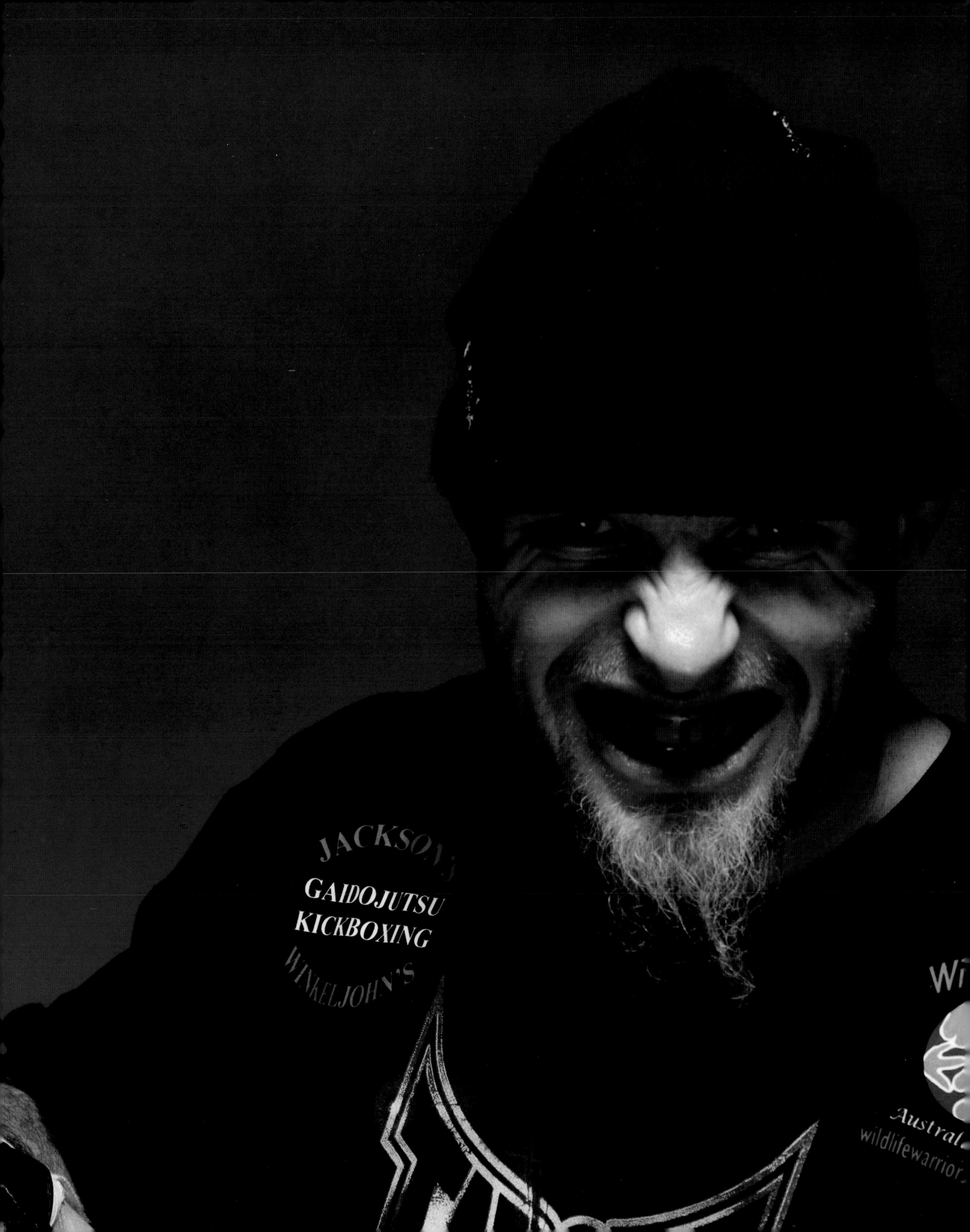
JACKSON'S
GAIDOJUTSU
KICKBOXING
WINKELJOHN'S

No me di cuenta de nada hasta que caminé por esas cortinas. Fue como "¡Cáspita, por fin la hice!" Luego me di cuenta que ya no estoy peleando por mí. Estoy peleando por todos. Por todos los que quieren esperanza, por esos estoy peleando.

ROGER HUERTA

Desna noga bolnica, lijeva noga groblje.   M I R K O   C R O   C O P

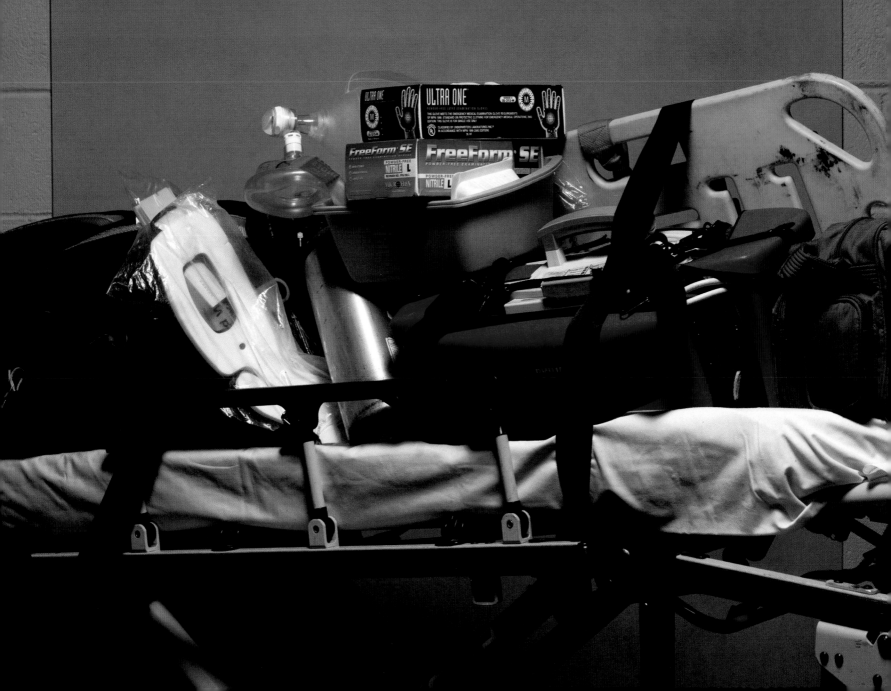

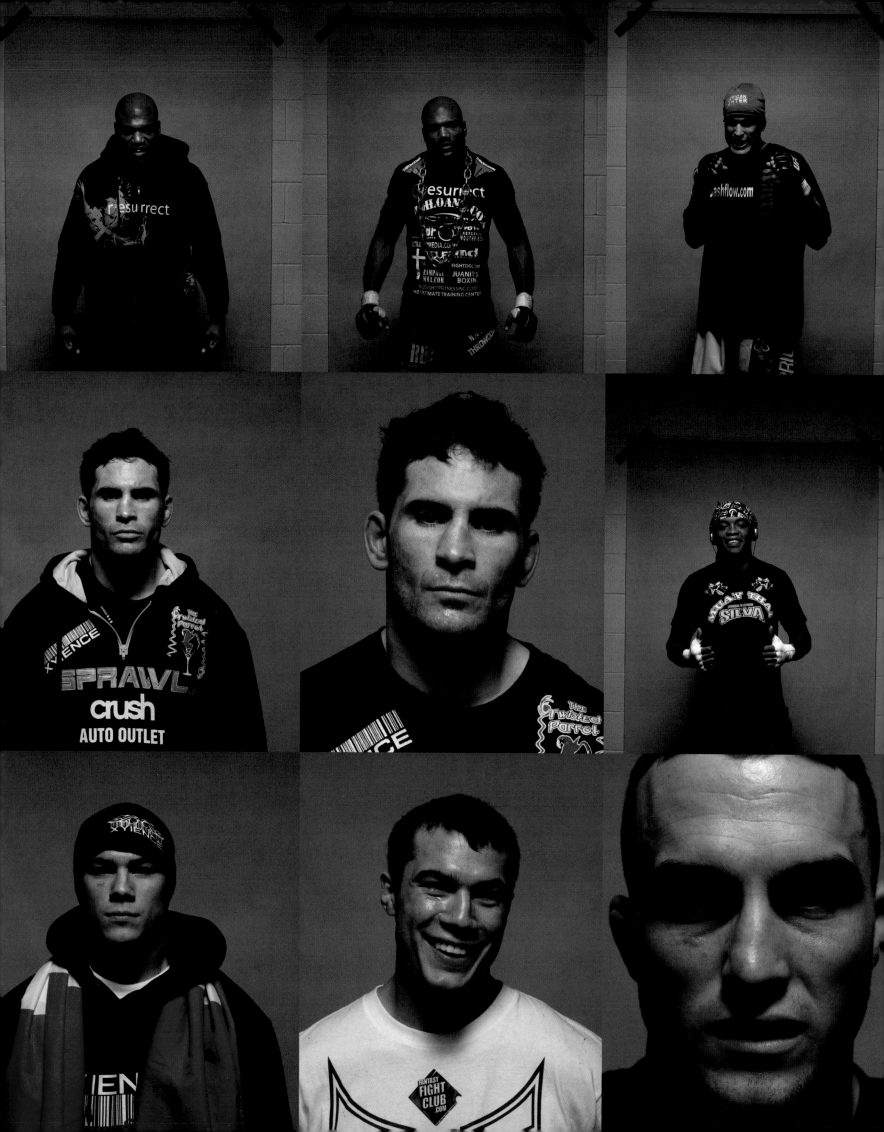

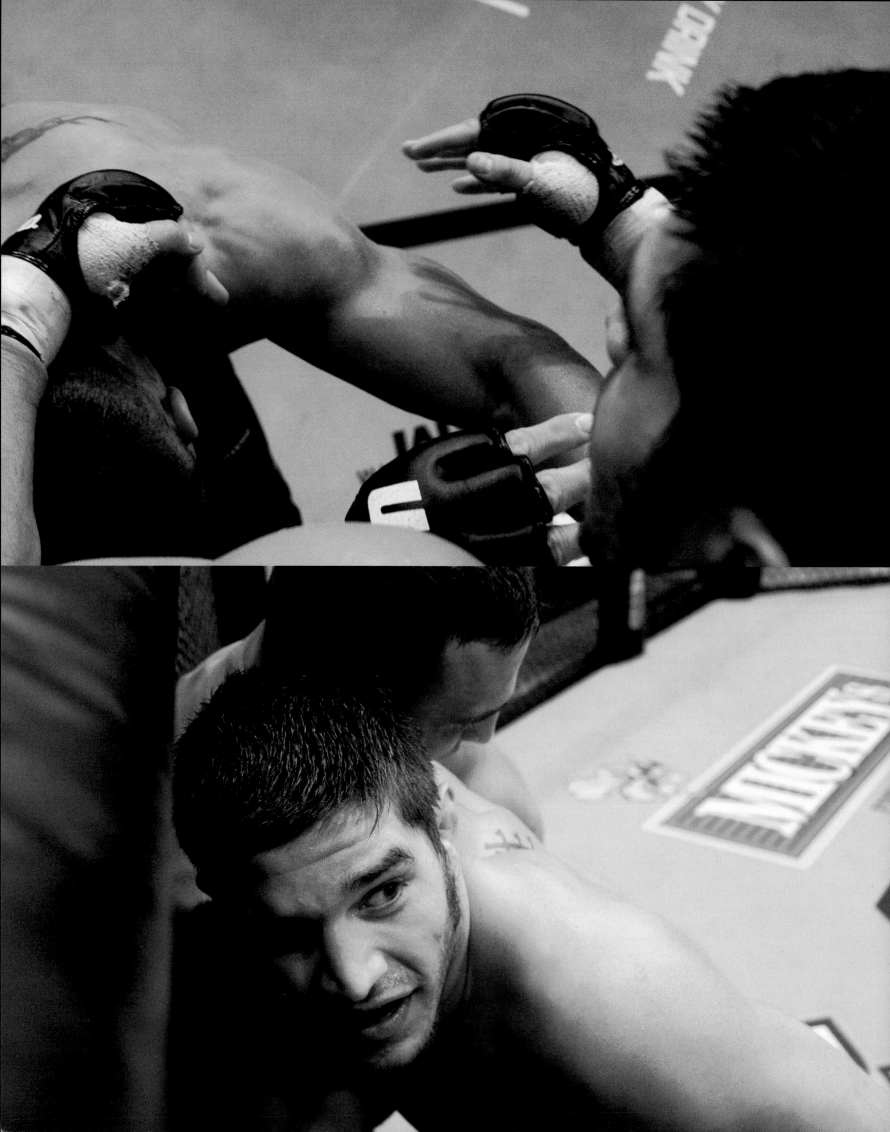

Mirko Cro Cop Vs. Eddie Sanchez, UFC 67
2/3/2007

Sem nervos. Nesse momento não tem aonde correr. Se você treinou, você treinou, se você não treinou, então você está ferrado.

ANDERSON SILVA

MICKEYS
FINE MALT LIQUOR
THE ULTRA PREMIUM
cran/razz • clear
XYIENCE
xyience
available at
amp'd mobile
TOYO TIRES
DRIVEN TO PERFORM
TAPOUT.COM
UFC.COM
NATIONWIDE ARENA
SHOOT
OTER

Chris Lytle Vs. Matt Hughes, UFC 68
3/3/2007

THE MAINE-IAC
TIM SYLVIA

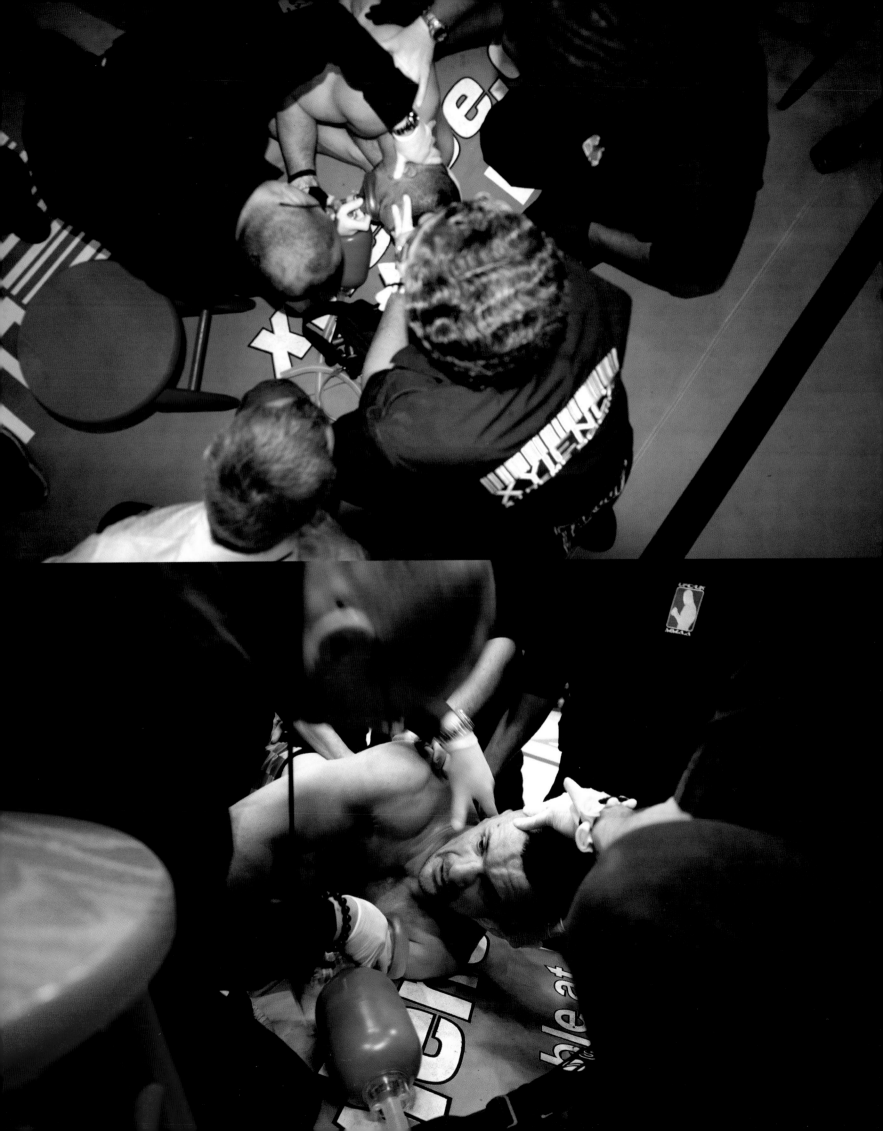

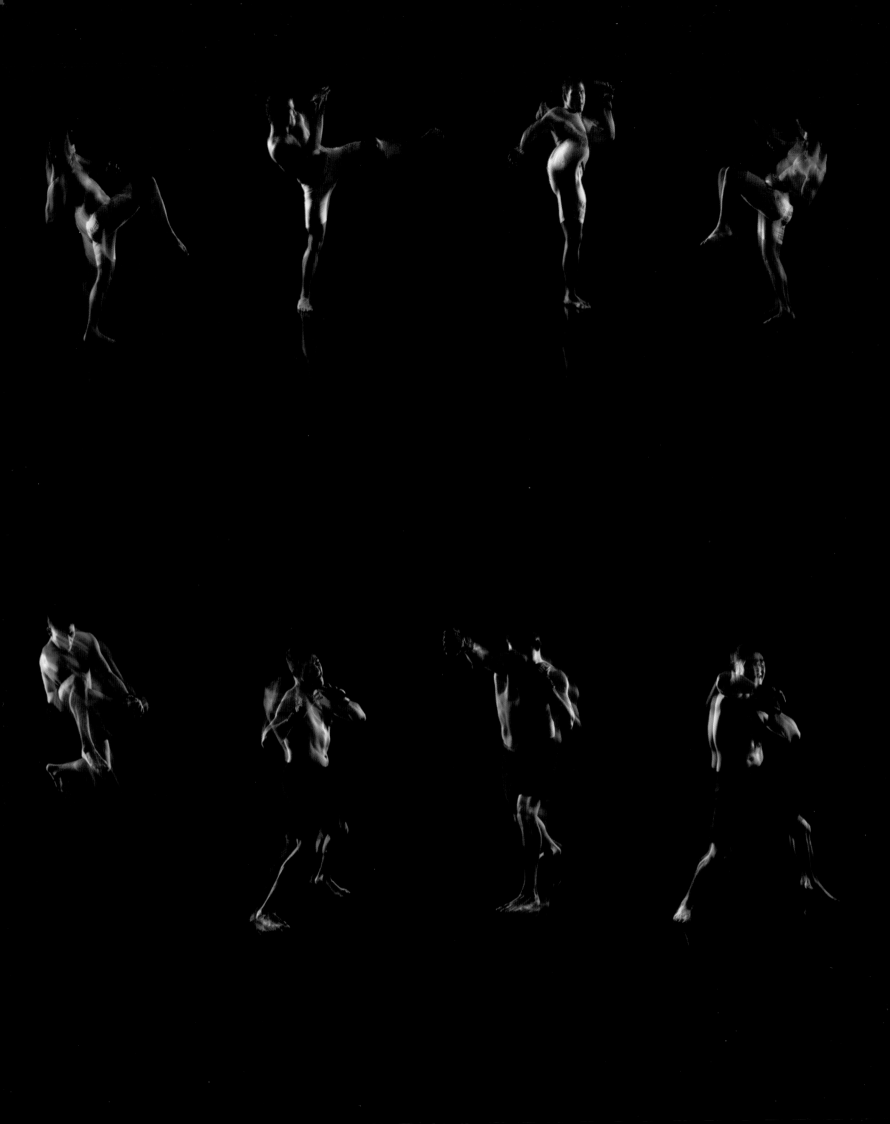

My mindset is, I'm gonna try to go where my opponent doesn't want to go—we'll see who can suffer the longest. That's basically it, and if he can outlast me in suffering, then he wins the fight.

RASHAD EVANS

I'm not gonna get in there having any doubt in my mind that I'm gonna win this fight. The only thing that takes the doubt out of my mind is that the harder I train, the more confident I get, and that makes me want to train all the time. I want to step in that cage and know that this guy doesn't have a chance.

SEAN SHERK

Ever since I can remember, I always loved fights. Whether it was sitting in front of the television watching boxing on Saturday afternoons when I was growing up or getting together with a bunch of friends to go to the arena to see a championship fight, there was nothing better than watching two fighters go toe-to-toe while matching wits and trying to prove who had the bigger heart.

To me, it was better than baseball, basketball or football, sports where you had teammates to help you out or take the blame when you lost. Fighting was a one-on-one sport, *mano e mano*, with no excuses. If you won, you took all the glory; you lost, you had no one to blame but yourself.

It was sport at its purest, but as the years went on, I saw boxing get engulfed and diluted by politics, in-fighting, and greed. I started to get disillusioned by the sport I loved, and it wasn't until I met some athletes competing in a sport called mixed martial arts that the love of combat sports came back for me like it did when I was growing up.

In this sport, which combined the disciplines of boxing, wrestling, Muay Thai, kickboxing, and Jiu-Jitsu, I not only saw the future, but I saw the understated artistry that only true fight fans can appreciate. It's something a lot of people can't see, and I could never really put my finger on what it is, but when I saw Kevin Lynch's photographs, I finally found something I could point to and say "that's it. That's what this sport is about."

So when we at the Ultimate Fighting Championship decided to move forward with the book project that became *Octagon*, there was no question who would be the photographer. And while Kevin's talent is obvious, his understanding of this sport and its athletes was another key factor in our decision, because let's face it – not everyone is willing to look past the misconceptions about mixed martial arts and give it the fair treatment it deserves.

It's been a long process to get to this point – for the UFC and for this book – but it was of the utmost importance to get it right, whether that meant unprecedented access to our events for Kevin, or having him capture our athletes at their most vulnerable, which was immediately before and after their fights. In combat sports, or any sport for that matter, vulnerability can be seen as weakness; but one look at the pictures in this book will show that behind the bruises and cuts and the defeated or triumphant eyes, there is strength. It's what these athletes are all about, and let me tell you, it takes

Started in 1993, the Ultimate Fighting Championship® (UFC®) brand is in its fourteenth year of operation as a professional mixed martial arts organization offering the premier series of MMA sports events.

The UFC organization follows a rich history and tradition of competitive MMA dating back to the Olympic Games in Athens. About 80 years ago, a Brazilian form of MMA known as Vale Tudo (anything goes) sparked local interest in the sport.

Then, the UFC organization brought MMA to the United States. The goal was to find "the Ultimate Fighting Champion" with a concept to have a tournament of the best athletes skilled in the various disciplines of all martial arts, including karate, jiu-jitsu, boxing, kickboxing, grappling, wrestling, sumo and other combat sports. The winner of the tournament would be crowned the champion.

Once the UFC brand was launched, MMA popularity surged in Brazil, followed by immense interest in Japan where these bouts became major events.

In January 2001, under the new ownership of Zuffa, LLC, the UFC brand completely restructured MMA into a highly organized and controlled combat sport. As a result, the UFC organization now offers twelve to fourteen live pay-per-view events annually through cable and satellite providers. UFC fight programs are also distributed internationally throughout the world, including broadcast on WOWOW, Inc. in Japan, MAIN EVENT in Australia, Globosat in Brazil and Bravo in the United Kingdom.

Response to the UFC brand of MMA has been tremendous, resulting in a fan base that has grown exponentially through the years.

Recently, a UFC event in Montreal, Canada attracted more than 22,000 people—the largest audience in North America to witness a mixed martial arts event. UFC popularity continues to reach new heights as the UFC organization and Spike TV Network extended its strategic partnership with additional seasons of the hit reality series *The Ultimate Fighter®*, as well as live *UFC® Fight Night™* events, and UFC: *Unleashed™*.

The UFC is the largest pay-per-view provider in the world and UFC programming is distrubuted in over 130 countries and territories.

The UFC organization is regulated and recognized by the world's most prestigious sports regulatory bodies including the California, Florida, Nevada, New Jersey, Ohio and Pennsylvania State Athletic Commissions. The UFC organization strives for the highest levels of safety and quality in all aspects of the sport.

Under the strong leadership of owners Frank Fertitta III and Lorenzo Fertitta, and expertise of President Dana White, the UFC brand continues to thrive across a spectrum of live event sports, television production and ancillary business development.

TRANSLATIONS

When you fight, you fight against your own mistakes. You're training and it's so good to have a challenge in your life – to climb the mountain.

VITOR BELFORT
(Portuguese) - Brazil

This is my house, I built it.

ROYCE GRACIE
(Portuguese) - Brazil

No nerves. At that moment there's nowhere to run. If you trained, you trained; if you didn't, you're screwed.

ANDERSON SILVA
(Portuguese) - Brazil

When I saw Royce Gracie in the first Ultimate Fighting Championship, it was like the Super Bowl of mixed martial arts. You can be a karate champion, judo champion, or jiu-jitsu champion, but when you're the ultimate fighting champion, you're the champion of everything all mixed together.

GEORGES ST-PIERRE
(French) - Canada

Right leg hospital; left leg cemetery

MIRKO CRO COP
(Croatian)

Pretty much anyone who steps into the Octagon as a contender is a threat. I take all of my opponents seriously, I respect all of them, and I realize that they don't get there by chance or by coincidence. There are reasons why people get an opportunity to fight for a title.

ANDREI ARLOVSKI
(Russian) – Belarus

This is really within me. It's a sport that allows me to challenge myself and follow the path of honor and the warrior spirit. My destiny was to be a fighter, so I'm happy and this is where I belong right now."

ALESSIO SAKARA
(Italian)

I was a boy, fighting guys in their 20's, 230 pounds of all muscle, and I broke their noses and choked them out in the first round. I never thought too much of it at the time. I was in high school. When I was 16, I fought a Gracie purple belt. He came in with his kids. He was 34 years old. No disrespect to him, but it wasn't even a fight; I played with him. He wore a judo gi, so all I did was grip and throw him. Finally, I knocked him down and got him in a rear naked choke, and I went to school the next day.

KARO PARISYAN
(Armenian)

Nothing hit me until I walked through those curtains. I was like 'wow, I finally made it.' Then it hit me that I'm not fighting for me anymore. I'm fighting for everyone. For anyone that wants hope, that's who I'm fighting for.

ROGER HUERTA
(Spanish) - Mexico

What is your favorite technique? Sorry, it's a secret.

KEITA NAKAMURA
(Japanese)

The mental side is everything. The techniques have to be flawless, but the mind has to be tough. It has to be more flawless and you can never give up. I would even sit here and say that I'm in the entertainment business and the fight game business, but I'm also in the making you quit business. That's what it's all about.

BJ PENN
(Hawaiian)

UFC 1: The Beginning – November 12, 1993 – McNichols Arena – Denver, CO

UFC 2: No Way Out – March 11, 1994 – Mammoth Gardens – Denver, CO

UFC 3: The American Dream – September 9, 1994 - Grady Cole Center – Charlotte, NC

UFC 4: Revenge of the Warriors – December 16, 1994 – Expo Square Pavilion –Tulsa, OK

UFC 5: Return of the Beast – April 4, 1995 – Independence Arena – Charlotte, NC

UFC 6: Clash of the Titans – July 14, 1995 – Casper Events Center – Casper, WY

UFC 7: Brawl in Buffalo – September 8, 1995 – Buffalo Memorial Auditorium – Buffalo, NY

Ultimate Ultimate 95 – December 16, 1995 – Mammoth Gardens – Denver, CO

UFC 8: David vs Goliath – February 16, 1996 – Ruben Rodriguez Coliseum – Bayamon, Puerto Rico

UFC 9: Motor City Madness – May 17, 1996 – Cobo Arena – Detroit, MI

UFC 10: The Tournament – July 12, 1996 – State Fair Arena – Birmingham, AL

UFC 11: The Proving Ground - September 20, 1996 – Augusta Civic Center – Augusta, GA

Ultimate Ultimate 96 – December 7, 1996 – State Fair Arena – Birmingham, AL

UFC 12: Judgment Day – February 7, 1997 - Dothan Civic Center – Dothan, AL

UFC 13: The Ultimate Force – May 30, 1997 – Augusta Civic Center – Augusta, GA

UFC 14: Showdown - July 27, 1997 – Boutwell Auditorium – Birmingham, AL

UFC 15: Collision Course – October 17, 1997 – Casino Magic - Bay St. Louis, MS

Ultimate Japan 1 - December 21, 1997 – Yokohama Arena – Yokohama, Japan

UFC 16: Battle in the Bayou – March 13, 1998 – Pontchartrain Center - New Orleans, LA

UFC 17: Redemption – May 15, 1998 – Mobile Civic Center – Mobile, AL

Ultimate Brazil – October 16, 1998 – Ginasio da Portuguesa – Sao Paulo, Brazil

UFC 18: Road to the Heavyweight Title – January 8, 1999 – Pontchartrain Center - New Orleans, LA

UFC 19: Young Guns – March 5, 1999 - Casino Magic - Bay St. Louis, MS

UFC 20: Battle for the Gold – May 7, 1999 - Boutwell Auditorium – Birmingham, AL

UFC 21: Return of the Champions – July 16, 1999 - Five Seasons Event Center - Cedar Rapids, IA

UFC 22: There Can Be Only One Champion – September 24, 1999 – Lake Charles Civic Center - Lake Charles, LA

UFC 23: Ultimate Japan 2 – November 19, 1999 - Tokyo Bay NK Hall – Tokyo, Japan

UFC 24: First Defense – March 10, 2000 - Lake Charles Civic Center - Lake Charles, LA

UFC 25: Ultimate Japan 3 - April 14, 2000 – Yoyogi National Gymnasium – Tokyo, Japan

UFC 26: Ultimate Field of Dreams – June 9, 2000 Five Seasons Event Center - Cedar Rapids, IA

UFC 27: Ultimate Bad Boyz – September 22, 2000 – Lakefront Arena - New Orleans, LA

UFC 28: High Stakes - November 17, 2000 – Trump Taj Mahal - Atlantic City, NJ

UFC 29: Defense of the Belts - December 16, 2000 – Differ Ariake Arena – Tokyo, Japan

UFC 30: Battle on the Boardwalk – February 23, 2001 - Trump Taj Mahal - Atlantic City, NJ

UFC 31: Locked and Loaded - May 4, 2001 - Trump Taj Mahal - Atlantic City, NJ

UFC 32: Showdown at the Meadowlands – June 29, 2001 – Continental Airlines Arena - East Rutherford NJ

UFC 33: Victory in Vegas – September 28, 2001 – Mandalay Bay Events Center - Las Vegas, NV

UFC 34: High Voltage - November 2, 2001 – MGM Grand - Las Vegas, NV

UFC 35: Throwdown – January 11, 2002 – Mohegan Sun Arena – Uncasville, CT

UFC 36: Worlds Collide – March 22, 2002 - MGM Grand - Las Vegas, NV

UFC 37: High Impact – May 10, 2002 – CenturyTel Center - Bossier City, LA

UFC 37.5: As Real As It Gets – June 22, 2002 – Bellagio - Las Vegas, NV

UFC 38: Brawl at the Hall – July 13, 2002 – Royal Albert Hall – London, England

UFC 39: The Warriors Return – September 27, 2002 - Mohegan Sun Arena – Uncasville, CT

UFC 40: Vendetta – November 22, 2002 - MGM Grand - Las Vegas, NV

UFC 41: Onslaught - February 28, 2003 – Boardwalk Hall - Atlantic City, NJ

UFC 42: Sudden Impact - April 25, 2003 – American Airlines Arena – Miami, FL

UFC 43: Meltdown - June 6, 2003 – Thomas and Mack Center - Las Vegas, NV

UFC 44: Undisputed - September 26, 2003 - Mandalay Bay Events Center - Las Vegas, NV

UFC 45: Revolution - November 21, 2003 - Mohegan Sun Arena – Uncasville, CT

UFC 46: Super Natural – January 31, 2004 - Mandalay Bay Events Center - Las Vegas, NV

UFC 47: It's On – April 2, 2004 - Mandalay Bay Events Center - Las Vegas, NV

UFC 48: Payback – June 19, 2004 - Mandalay Bay Events Center - Las Vegas, NV

UFC 49: Unfinished Business – August 21, 2004 - MGM Grand - Las Vegas, NV

UFC 50: The War of '04 - October 22, 2004 - Boardwalk Hall - Atlantic City, NJ

UFC 51: Super Saturday – February 5, 2005 - Mandalay Bay Events Center - Las Vegas, NV

The Ultimate Fighter 1 – April 9, 2005 – Cox Pavilion - Las Vegas, NV

UFC 52: Couture vs. Liddell 2 – April 16, 2005 - MGM Grand - Las Vegas, NV

UFC 53: Heavy Hitters - June 4, 2005 - Boardwalk Hall - Atlantic City, NJ

Ultimate Fight Night 1 – August 6, 2005 - Cox Pavilion - Las Vegas, NV

UFC 54: Boiling Point – August 20, 2005 - MGM Grand - Las Vegas, NV

The Ultimate Fighter 2 Finale – September 5, 2005 - Hard Rock Hotel and Casino - Las Vegas, NV

Ultimate Fight Night 2 – October 3, 2005 – Hard Rock Hotel and Casino - Las Vegas, NV

UFC 55: Fury - October 7, 2005 - Mohegan Sun Arena – Uncasville, CT

UFC 56: Full Force - November 19, 2005 - MGM Grand - Las Vegas, NV

Ultimate Fight Night 3 – January 16, 2006 - Hard Rock Hotel and Casino - Las Vegas, NV

UFC 57: Liddell vs. Couture 3 – February 4, 2006 - Mandalay Bay Events Center - Las Vegas, NV

UFC 58: USA vs. Canada – March 4, 2006 - Mandalay Bay Events Center - Las Vegas, NV

Ultimate Fight Night 4 – April 6, 2006 - Hard Rock Hotel and Casino - Las Vegas, NV

UFC 59: Reality Check – April 15, 2006 - Arrowhead Pond – Anaheim, CA

UFC 60: Hughes vs. Gracie – May 27, 2006 – Staples Center - Los Angeles, CA

The Ultimate Fighter 3 Finale – June 24, 2006 - Hard Rock Hotel and Casino - Las Vegas, NV

Ultimate Fight Night 5 – June 28, 2006 - Hard Rock Hotel and Casino - Las Vegas, NV

UFC 61: Bitter Rivals – July 8, 2006 - Mandalay Bay Events Center - Las Vegas, NV

Ultimate Fight Night 6 – August 27, 2006 – Red Rock Resort Spa and Casino - Las Vegas, NV

UFC 62: Liddell vs. Sobral – August 26, 2006 - Mandalay Bay Events Center - Las Vegas, NV

UFC 63: Penn vs. Hughes – September 23, 2006 - Arrowhead Pond – Anaheim, CA

UFC Fight Night – Ortiz vs Shamrock 3 – October 10, 2006 – Seminole Hard Rock Live Arena – Hollywood, FL

UFC 64: Unstoppable – October 14, 2006 - Mandalay Bay Events Center - Las Vegas, NV

The Ultimate Fighter 4 Finale – November 11, 2006 - Hard Rock Hotel and Casino - Las Vegas, NV

UFC 65: Bad Intentions – November 18, 2006 – Arco Arena – Sacramento, CA

Ultimate Fight Night 7 – December 13, 2006 - MCAS Miramar - San Diego, CA

UFC 66: Liddell vs. Ortiz 2 – December 30, 2006 - MGM Grand - Las Vegas, NV

UFC Fight Night 8 – January 25, 2007 Seminole Hard Rock Live Arena – Hollywood, FL

UFC 67: All or Nothing – February 3, 2007 - Mandalay Bay Events Center - Las Vegas, NV

UFC 68: The Uprising – March 3, 2007 – Nationwide Arena – Columbus, OH

UFC Fight Night 9 – April 5, 2007 – The Palms - Las Vegas, NV

UFC 69: Shootout – April 7, 2007 – Toyota Center – Houston, TX

UFC 70: Nations Collide – April 21, 2007 – MEN Arena – Manchester, England

Gatefolds, outside page

Chuck Liddell series, Las Vegas, NV
1/15/04

Gatefolds, inside page

First row: Mark Weir, Phillip Miller, Vladimir Matyushenko, Andrei Arlovski, Eddie Ruiz, Matt Lindland, Falaniko Vitale, Frank Mir, Ian Freeman, Marvin Eastman, Vitor Belfort, Tank Abbott, Kimo Leopoldo, Chuck Liddell, Randy Couture, Jeff Curran, Matt Serra, Georges St. Pierre, Wade Shipp

Second row: Andrei Arlovski, Genki Sudo, Wes Sims, Mike Kyle, Mike Brown, Nick Diaz, Robbie Lawler, Yves Edwards, Matt Serra, Ivan Menjivar, Georges St. Pierre, Jay Hieron, Trevor Prangley, Curtis Stout, Dennis Hallman, Phil Baroni, Frank Mir, Ken Shamrock, Chris Lytle,

Third row: Ronald Jhun, Matt Lindland, David Terrell, Joe Doerksen, Joe Riggs, Josh Thomson, Yves Edwards, Nick Diaz, Karo Parisyan, Mike Kyle, Justin Eilers, Vernon White, Chuck Liddell, Randy Couture, Tony Fryklund, Ivan Salaverry, Jorge Rivera, Rich Franklin, Travis Lutter

Fourth row: Frank Trigg, Robbie Lawler, Evan Tanner, Georges St. Pierre, Patrick Cote, Nate Quarry, Lodune Sincaid, Josh Koscheck, Sam Hoger, Jason Thacker, Chris Leben, Mike Swick, Kenny Florian, Diego Sanchez, Stephan Bonnar, Forrest Griffin, Ken Shamrock, Ivan Salaverry, Travis Lutter

Fifth row: Matt Lindland, Mike Van Arsdale, Patrick Cote, Joe Doerksen, Georges St. Pierre, Frank Trigg, Matt Hughes, Chuck Liddell, Nate Quarry, Kenny Florian, Alex Karalexis, Stephan Bonnar, Alessio Sakara, Randy Couture, Chuck Liddell, Jeremy Horn, Fabiano Scherner, Gabriel Gonzaga, Alessio Sakara

Sixth row: Matt Wiman, Spencer Fisher, John Alessio, Diego Sanchez, Joe Riggs, Mike Swick, Brandon Vera, Matt Hughes, Gilbert Aldana, Cheick Kongo, Ken Shamrock, Andrei Arlovski, Tim Sylvia, Rashad Evans, Mike Swick, Thales Leites, Martin Kampmann, Gideon Ray, Pete Sell

Seventh row: Scott Smith, Jeremy Jackson, Edwin Dewees, Jorge Rivera, Rich Clementi, Din Thomas, Patrick Cote, Travis Lutter, Chris Lytle, Matt Serra, Hector Ramirez, James Irvin, Josh Shockman, Jake O'Brien, Antoni Hardonk, Gleison Tibau, Nick Diaz, Dokonjonosuke Mishima, Joe Stevenson

Eighth row: Brandon Vera, Jeff Monson, Tim Sylvia, Matt Hughes, Georges St. Pierre, Steve Byrnes, Logan Clark, Keita Nakamura, Brock Larson, Dave Menne, Luigi Fioravanti, Alan Belcher, Victor Valimaki, David Heath, Shonie Carter, Marcus Davis, Drew Fickett, Karo Parisyan, Jeff Joslin, Josh Koscheck

Ninth row: Diego Sanchez, Carmelo Marrero, Gabriel Gonzaga, Tony DeSouza, Thiago Alves, Michael Bisping, Chris Leben, Jason MacDonald, Marcio Cruz, Andrei Arlovski, Forrest Griffin, Keith Jardine, Chuck Liddell, Tyson Griffin, Frank Edgar, Jorge Rivera, Terry Martin, Scott Smith, Patrick Cote

Tenth row: Marvin Eastman, Quinton Jackson, Eddie Sanchez, Mirko Cro Cop, John Halverson, Roger Huerta, Travis Lutter, Anderson Silva, Jason Dent, Gleison Tibau, Luigi Fioravanti, Jon Fitch, Rex Holman, Matt Hamill, Jason Lambert, Jason MacDonald, Rich Franklin, Chris Lytle, Matt Hughes, Tim Sylvia

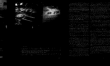

P002-003
...en Shamrock in the Octagon™,
...s Vegas,NV
.../22/02

P004-005
Arena before the event, UFC 68,
Nationwide Arena, Columbus, OH
3/3/07

P006-007
B.J. Penn triptych, Las Vegas,
NV
1/15/04

P008-009
Andrei Arlovski triptych. Las
Vegas, NV
1/15/04

P010-011
Melvin Guillard vs. Rick Davis,
UFC 60, Staples Center, Los
Angeles, CA
5/27/06

P012-013
Randy and Chuck bronze,
Los Angeles, CA
11/23/04

P014-015
Octagon after UFC 49, MGM
Grand, Las Vegas, NV
8/21/04

P016-017
...att Hughes flag,
...s Angeles, CA
...23/04

P018-019
Chuck Liddell close-up after UFC
43, Thomas and Mack Center,
Las Vegas, NV
6/6/03

P020-021
Phillip Miller before and after
UFC 40, MGM Grand, Las
Vegas, NV
11/22/02

P022-023
Mark Weir before and after UFC
40, MGM Grand, Las Vegas, NV
11/22/02

P024-025
Ken Shamrock after UFC 40,
MGM Grand, Las Vegas, NV
11/22/02

P026-027
Tito Ortiz vs. Ken Shamrock, UFC
40, MGM Grand, Las Vegas, NV
11/22/02

P028-029
Chuck Liddell before and after
UFC 43, Thomas and Mack
Center, Las Vegas, NV
6/6/03

P030-031
...arvin Eastman before and
...ter UFC 43, Thomas and Mack
...nter, Las Vegas, NV
6/03

P032-034
Ian Freeman before and after
UFC 43, Thomas and Mack
Center, Las Vegas, NV
6/6/03

P035-036
Top left: Falaniko Vitale, Top right: Eddie Ruiz, Bottom left: Kimo
Leopoldo, Bottom right: Tank Abbott, before and after UFC 43,
Thomas and Mack Center, Las Vegas, NV
6/6/03

P037-038
Frank Mir, locker room, UFC 43,
Thomas and Mack Center, Las
Vegas, NV
6/6/03

P039-040
Kimo Leopoldo vs. Tank Abbott,
UFC 43, Thomas and Mack
Center, Las Vegas, NV
6/6/03

P041-044
Pedro Rizzo vs. Tra Telligman,
UFC 43, Thomas and Mack
Center, Las Vegas, NV
6/6/03

P045-046
Matt Lindland vs. Falaniko Vitale,
UFC 43, Thomas and Mack
Center, Las Vegas, NV
6/6/03

P047-050
Chuck Liddell vs. Randy Couture,
UFC 43, Thomas and Mack
Center, Las Vegas, NV
6/6/03

P051-052
Georges St. Pierre before and
after UFC 46, Mandalay Bay
Events Center, Las Vegas, NV
1/31/04

P053-054
Top: Jeff Curran, Bottom: Matt
Serra, before and after UFC 46,
Mandalay Bay Events Center, Las
Vegas, NV
1/31/04

P055-056
Left: B.J. Penn, Right: Frank
Mir, after UFC 46, Mandalay Bay
Events Center, Las Vegas, NV
1/31/04

P057-062
...att Hughes vs. B.J. Penn, UFC
...6, Mandalay Bay Events Center,
...s Vegas, NV
...31/04

P063-064
Karo Parisyan vs. Georges St.
Pierre, UFC 46, Mandalay Bay
Events Center, Las Vegas, NV
1/31/04

P065-066
Frank Mir vs. Wes Sims, UFC 46,
Mandalay Bay Events Center, Las
Vegas, NV
1/31/04

P067-068
Vitor Belfort vs. Randy Couture,
UFC 46, Mandalay Bay Events
Center, Las Vegas, NV
1/31/04

P069-070
Wesley Correira before and after
UFC 47, Mandalay Bay Events
Center, Las Vegas, NV
4/2/04

P071-072
...ndrei Arlovski before and after
...FC 47, Mandalay Bay Events
...nter, Las Vegas, NV
...2/04

P073-074
Locker room before and after
UFC 47, Mandalay Bay Events
Center, Las Vegas, NV
4/2/04

P075-076
Wes Sims before and after UFC
47, Mandalay Bay Events Center,
Las Vegas, NV
4/2/04

P077-078
Top left: Wade Shipp, Top right: Yves Edwards, Bottom left: Genki
Sudo, Bottom right: Mike Kyle, before and after UFC 47, Mandalay
Bay Events Center, Las Vegas, NV
4/2/04

P079-082
Chuck Liddell vs. Tito Ortiz, UFC
47, Mandalay Bay Events Center,
Las Vegas, NV
4/2/04

P096-097
Top left: Phil Baroni, Top right: Ivan Menjivar, Bottom left: Curtis Stout, Bottom right: Trevor Prangley, before and after UFC 48, Mandalay Bay Events Center, Las Vegas, NV
6/19/04

P098: Top left: Chris Lytle, Top right: Joe Riggs, Center left: Chuck Liddell, Center right: Josh Thomson, Bottom left: Mike Kyle, Bottom right: Nick Diaz
P099: Top left: Vernon White, Top right: Matt Lindland, Center left: Ronald Jhun, Center right: David Terrell, Bottom left: Karo Parisyan, Bottom right: Yves Edwards Before and after UFC 49, MGM Grand, Las Vegas, NV
8/21/04

P100-101
Joe Doerksen before and after UFC 49, MGM Grand, Las Vegas, NV
8/21/04

P102-103
Left: Randy Couture
Right: Chuck Liddell vs. Vernon White UFC 49, MGM Grand, Las Vegas, NV
8/21/04

P104-105
Marvin Eastman vs. Travis Lutter, UFC 50, Boardwalk Hall, Atlantic City, NJ
10/22/04

P106-107
Travis Lutter before and after UFC 50, Boardwalk Hall, Atlantic City, NJ
10/22/04

P108-109
Tony Fryklund before and after UFC 50, Boardwalk Hall, Atlantic City, NJ
10/22/04

P110-111
Rich Franklin before and after UFC 50, Boardwalk Hall, Atlantic City, NJ
10/22/04

P112-113
Jorge Rivera before and after UFC 50, Boardwalk Hall, Atlantic City, NJ
10/22/04

P114-115
Georges St. Pierre before and after UFC 50 Boardwalk Hall, Atlantic City, NJ
10/22/04

P116
Matt Hughes after UFC 50 Boardwalk Hall, Atlantic City, NJ
10/22/04

P118-119
Top Left: Ivan Salaverry, Top Right: Evan Tanner, Bottom Left: Patrick Cote. Bottom Right: Robbie Lawler, before and after UFC 50, Boardwalk Hall, Atlantic City, NJ
10/22/04

P120-121
Frank Trigg, UFC 50, Boardwalk Hall, Atlantic City, NJ
10/22/04

P122: Top: Forrest Griffin, Bottom: Stephan Bonnar
P123: First row: Chris Leben, Lodune Sincaid, Second row: Sam Hoger, Jason Thacker, Third row: Diego Sanchez, Kenny Florian, Fourth row: Mike Swick, Josh Koscheck Before and after The Ultimate Fighter 1 Finale, Cox Pavilion, Las Vegas, NV
4/9/05

P124-125
Diego Sanchez vs. Kenny Florian, The Ultimate Fighter 1 Finale, Cox Pavilion, Las Vegas, NV
4/9/05

P126-127
Forrest Griffin vs. Stephan Bonnar, The Ultimate Fighter 1 Finale, Cox Pavilion, Las Vegas, NV
4/9/05

P128-131
Forrest Griffin vs. Stephan Bonnar, The Ultimate Fighter 1 Finale, Cox Pavilion, Las Vegas, NV
4/9/05

P132-141
Randy Couture vs. Chuck Liddell, UFC 52, MGM Grand, Las Vegas, NV
4/16/05

P142-143
Top left: Chuck Liddell, Top right: Matt Hughes, Bottom left: Georges St. Pierre, Bottom right: Frank Trigg, before and after UFC 52, MGM Grand, Las Vegas, NV
4/16/05

P144-145
Alex Karalexis before and after UFC Fight Night 3, Hard Rock Hotel and Casino, Las Vegas, NV
1/16/06

P146-147
Chuck Liddell vs. Randy Couture, UFC 57, Mandalay Bay Events Center, Las Vegas, NV
2/4/06

P148-149
Chuck Liddell before and after UFC 57, Mandalay Bay Events Center, Las Vegas, NV
2/4/06

P150-151
Alessio Sakara before and after UFC 57, Mandalay Bay Events Center, Las Vegas, NV
2/4/06

P152-153
Matt Hughes and Royce Gracie before UFC 60, Staples Center, Los Angeles, CA
5/27/06

P154-155
Diego Sanchez before and after UFC 60, Staples Center, Los Angeles, CA
5/27/06

P156-157
Top left: Mike Swick, Top right: Fabiano Scherner, Bottom left: Jeremy Horn, Bottom right: John Alessio, before and after UFC 60, Staples Center, Los Angeles, CA
5/27/06

P158-159
First row, from left: Gabriel Gonzaga, Spencer Fisher, Matt Wiman; Second row, from left: Dean Lister, Chael Sonnen, Assuerio Silva; Third row, from left: Alessio Sakara, Joe Riggs, Brandon Vera, before and after UFC 60, Staples Center, Los Angeles, CA
5/27/06

P160-161
Matt Wiman, UFC 60, Staples Center, Los Angeles, CA
5/27/06

P162-163
Diego Sanchez vs. John Alessio, UFC 60, Staples Center, Los Angeles, CA
5/27/06

P178-179
Hermes Franca vs. Joe Jordan, UFC 61, Mandalay Bay Events Center, Las Vegas, NV
7/8/06

P180-181
Tito Ortiz vs. Ken Shamrock, UFC 61, Mandalay Bay Events Center, Las Vegas, NV
7/8/06

P182-183
Yves Edwards vs. Joe Stevenson, UFC 61, Mandalay Bay Events Center, Las Vegas, NV
7/8/06

P184-185
Andrei Arlovski diptych, UFC 61, Mandalay Bay Events Center, Las Vegas, NV
7/8/06

P186-187
Top left: Andrei Arlovski, Top right: Ken Shamrock, Bottom left: Cheick Kongo, Bottom right: Tim Sylvia, before and after UFC 61, Mandalay Bay Events Center, Las Vegas, NV

P188-189
B.J. Penn and Mike Swick before and after UFC 63, Arrowhead Pond, Anaheim, CA
9/23/06

P190-191
Rashad Evans before and after UFC 63, Arrowhead Pond, Anaheim, CA
9/23/06

P192-193
Jason Dent and Jorge Gurgel after UFC 63, Arrowhead Pond, Anaheim, CA
9/23/06

P194-197
Matt Hughes vs. B.J. Penn, UFC 63, Arrowhead Pond, Anaheim, CA
9/23/06

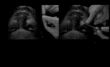

P198-199
The Ultimate Fighter 4 Finale, locker rooms, Hard Rock Hotel and Casino, Las Vegas, NV
11/11/06

P200-201
Scott Smith diptych, The Ultimate Fighter 4 Finale, Hard Rock Hotel and Casino, Las Vegas, NV
11/11/06

P202-203
Pete Sell close-up after The Ultimate Fighter 4 Finale, Hard Rock Hotel and Casino, Las Vegas, NV
11/11/06

P204-205
Thales Leites before and after The Ultimate Fighter 4 Finale, Hard Rock Hotel and Casino, Las Vegas, NV
11/11/06

P206-207
Din Thomas before and after The Ultimate Fighter 4 Finale, Hard Rock Hotel and Casino, Las Vegas, NV
11/11/06

P208-209
Martin Kampmann before and after The Ultimate Fighter 4 Finale, Hard Rock Hotel and Casino, Las Vegas, NV
11/11/06

P210-211
First row, from left: Travis Lutter, Pete Spratt, Chris Lytle; Second row, from left: Edwin Dewees, Scott Smith, Patrick Cote; Third row, from left: Matt Serra, Charles McCarthy, Rich Clementi, before and after The Ultimate Fighter 4 Finale, Hard Rock Hotel and Casino, Las Vegas, NV
11/11/06

P212-213
Jeff Monson before and after UFC 65, ARCO Arena, Sacramento, CA
11/18/06

P214-215
Tim Sylvia before and after UFC 65, ARCO Arena, Sacramento, CA
11/18/06

P216-217
Matt Hughes before and after UFC 65, ARCO Arena, Sacramento, CA
11/18/06

P218-219
Georges St. Pierre before and after UFC 65, ARCO Arena, Sacramento, CA
11/18/06

P220-221
First row, from left: Sherman Pendergarst, Brandon Vera, Jake O'Brien; Second row, from left: Joe Stevenson, Josh Shockman, Dokonjonosuke Mishima; Third row, from left: Gleison Tibau, James Irvin, Nick Diaz, before and after UFC 65, ARCO Arena, Sacramento, CA
11/18/06

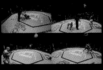

P222-223
Top: James Irvin vs. Hector Ramirez Bottom: Tim Sylvia vs. Jeff Monson UFC 65, ARCO Arena, Sacramento, CA
11/18/06

P224-225
Tim Sylvia vs. Jeff Monson, UFC 65, ARCO Arena, Sacramento, CA
11/18/06

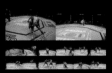

P226-227
Matt Hughes vs. Georges St. Pierre, UFC 65, ARCO Arena, Sacramento, CA
11/18/06

P228-229
UFC Fight Night 7, MCAS Miramar, San Diego, CA
12/13/06

P230-231
Drew Fickett before and after UFC Fight Night, MCAS Miramar, San Diego, CA
12/13/06

P232-233
Karo Parisyan, UFC Fight Night 7, MCAS Miramar, San Diego, CA
12/13/06

P234-235
First row, from left: Diego Sanchez, Dave Menne, Josh Koscheck; Second row, from left: Brock Larson, Marcus Davis, Jeff Joslin; Third row, from left: David Heath, Victor Valimaki, Shonie Carter, UFC Fight Night 7, MCAS Miramar, San Diego, CA
12/13/06

P236: Luigi Fioravanti
P237: Keita Nakamura
UFC Fight Night 7, MCAS Miramar, San Diego, CA
12/13/06

P238-239
MCM Arena, before UFC Fight Night 7, MCAS Miramar, San Diego, CA
12/13/06

P240-243
MCM Arena, UFC Fight Night 7, MCAS Miramar, San Diego, CA
12/13/06

P244-245
Jeff Joslin vs. Josh Koscheck, UFC Fight Night 7, MCAS Miramar, San Diego, CA
12/13/06

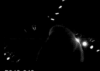

P246-247
Drew Fickett vs. Karo Parisyan, UFC Fight Night 7, MCAS Miramar, San Diego, CA
12/13/06

P248-249
Michael Bisping UFC 66, MGM Grand, Las Vegas, NV
12/30/06

P250-251
Eric Schafer vs. Michael Bisping, UFC 66, MGM Grand, Las Vegas, NV
12/30/06

P252-255
Andrei Arlovski vs. Marcio Cruz, UFC 66, MGM Grand, Las Vegas, NV
12/30/06

P256-257
Jason MacDonald vs. Chris Leben, UFC 66, MGM Grand, Las Vegas, NV
12/30/06

P258-259
Keith Jardine vs. Forrest Griffin, UFC 66, MGM Grand, Las Vegas, NV
12/30/06

P260-267
Chuck Liddell vs. Tito Ortiz, MGM Grand, UFC 66, Las Vegas, NV
12/30/06

P268-269
Tony DeSouza before and after
UFC 66, MGM Grand, Las
Vegas, NV
12/30/06

P270-271
Gabriel Gonzaga before and
after UFC 66, MGM Grand, Las
Vegas, NV
12/30/06

P272-273
Chuck Liddell before and after
UFC 66, MGM Grand, Las
Vegas, NV
12/30/06

P274-275
First row, from left: Thiago Alves, Michael Bisping, Jason MacDonald;
Second row, from left: Carmelo Marrero, Chris Leben, Marcio Cruz; Third
row, from left: Andrei Arlovski, Eric Schafer, Yushin Okami, Christian
Wellisch, Rory Singer, before and after UFC 66, MGM Grand, Las Vegas, NV
12/30/06

P276-277
Forrest Griffin before and after
UFC 66, MGM Grand, Las
Vegas, NV
12/30/06

P278-279
Keith Jardine before and after
UFC 66, MGM
Grand, Las Vegas, NV
12/30/06

P280: Quinton Jackson
P281: Eddie Sanchez
UFC 67, Mandalay Bay Events
Center, Las Vegas, NV
2/3/07

P282: Roger Huerta
P283: Terry Martin UFC 67,
Mandalay Bay Events Center, Las
Vegas, NV
2/3/07

P284: Mirko Cro Cop
P285: Ambulance stretcher
UFC 67, Mandalay Bay Events
Center, Las Vegas, NV
2/3/07

P286-287
Patrick Cote before and after UFC
67, Mandalay Bay Events Center,
Las Vegas, NV
2/3/07

P288-289
First row, from left: Quinton Jackson, Sam Hoger, Frank Edgar; Second
row, from left: John Halverson, Anderson Silva, Marvin Eastman; Third
row, from left: Roger Huerta, Scott Smith, Travis Lutter, before and
after UFC 67, Mandalay Bay Events Center, Las Vegas, NV
2/3/07

P290
Top left: Dustin Hazelett, Top
right: Diego Saraiva, Bottom left:
Eddie Sanchez, Bottom right:
Lyoto Machida, after UFC 67

P291
Top: Terry Martin, Bottom: Jorge
Rivera Before and after UFC 67,
Mandalay Bay Events Center, Las
Vegas, NV
2/3/07

P292-297
Patrick Cote vs. Scott Smith,
UFC 67, Mandalay Bay Events
Center, Las Vegas, NV
2/3/07

P298-301
Mirko Cro Cop vs. Eddie
Sanchez, UFC 67, Mandalay Bay
Events Center, Las Vegas, NV
2/3/07

P302: Marvin Eastman
P303: Quinton Jackson
UFC 67, Mandalay Bay Events
Center, Las Vegas, NV
2/3/07

P304-305
Anderson Silva vs. Travis Lutter,
UFC 67, Mandalay Bay Events
Center, Las Vegas, NV
2/3/07

P306-309
Jason Gilliam vs. Jamie Varner,
UFC 68, Nationwide Arena,
Columbus, OH
3/3/07

P310-311
Tim Sylvia vs. Randy Couture,
UFC 68, Nationwide Arena,
Columbus, OH
3/3/07

P312-313
Chris Lytle vs. Matt Hughes,
UFC 68, Nationwide Arena,
Columbus, OH
3/3/07

P314-317
Tim Sylvia vs. Randy Couture,
UFC 68, Nationwide Arena,
Columbus, OH
3/3/07

P318-319
Top left: Jon Fitch, Top right: Rich Franklin, Bottom left: Jason
MacDonald, Bottom right: Martin Kampmann, before and after UFC
68, Nationwide Arena, Columbus, OH
3/3/07

P320-321
First row, from left: Jason Lambert, Jason Gilliam, Jason Dent;
Second row, from left: Matt Hamill, Gleison Tibau, Chris Lytle; Third
row, from left: Jamie Varner, Rex Holman, Luigi Fioravanti, before
and after UFC 68, Nationwide Arena, Columbus, OH
3/3/07

P322-323
Matt Hughes before and after
UFC 68, Nationwide Arena,
Columbus, OH
3/3/07

P324-325
Tim Sylvia before and after
UFC 68, Nationwide Arena,
Columbus, OH
3/3/07

P327
"We Are All One," UFC 47,
Mandalay Bay Events Center, Las
Vegas, NV
4/2/04

 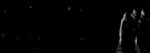    

P328-329 First row, from left: Edilberto Crocota, Paul Taylor, Matt Grice, Dennis Siver; Second row, from
left: Victor Valimaki, Alessio Sakara, David Lee; Third row, from left: Fabricio Werdum, Junior Assuncao,
Jess Liaudin, Mirko Cro Cop, Gabriel Gonzaga; Fourth row, from left: Gabriel Gonzaga, Andrei Arlovski,
Elvis Sinosic, Cheick Kongo; Fifth row, from left: Michael Bisping, David Heath, Assuerio Silva, Terry Etim,
Lyoto Machida, before and after UFC 70, MEN Arena, Manchester, England
4/21/07

P330-331
David Heath vs. Lyoto Machida,
UFC 70, MEN
Arena, Manchester, England
4/21/07

P332-333
Michael Bisping vs. Elvis
Sinosic, UFC 70, MEN Arena,
Manchester, England
4/21/07

P334-337
Mirko Cro Cop vs. Gabriel
Gonzaga, UFC 70, MEN Arena,
Manchester, England
4/21/07

OCTAGON™

Photography by **Kevin Lynch**
Foreword by **David Mamet** / Essay by **Dave Hickey**
Introduction by **Lorenzo Fertitta** / Afterword by **Dana White**

Limited edition, clothbound book, with more than 800 photographs, and handmade leather-bound clamshell box (20.5 x 26 inches), documenting a four-year history of the Ultimate Fighting Championship®. Edition of 600, with 150 Deluxe Editions including a limited edition photograph. Also available are 22 unique limited edition photographs by Kevin Lynch.

Please contact **702.588.5523** for more information.

Published by Zuffa, LLC.

WWW.OCTAGON-BOOK.COM

ACKNOWLEDGMENTS

You know you are on to something when you have people like Frank and Lorenzo Fertitta, Dana White, Dave Hickey, and David Mamet collaborating with you on a project like this one. The book starts taking on its own life, and sooner or later, so many people are involved and they become instrumental in elevating and shaping the project into a reality. The four years it took has been an extraordinary experience for me.

Special thanks to all the athletes of the UFC® for letting me share these personal moments with them. I admire you all for your courage, talent, and dedication to this great sport.

I'm forever indebted to Frank and Lorenzo Fertitta and Dana White for their keen vision and unprecedented support in producing and guiding this book all the way through to its completion.

My utmost respect and heartfelt thanks go to Kirk Hendrick and Craig Borsari for believing in this project.

Jaime Pollack for his great vision and support, which were instrumental in bringing this project from conception to reality.

Jim Byrne for his phenomenal marketing skills and for protecting the integrity of this project.

Thank you to the dedicated staff of the UFC:

Donna Marcolini for always helping with her superb organizational contributions;

Burt Watson for his wisdom and friendship and his great support team behind the scenes; and Greg Hendrick, Jennifer Wenk, Sean Shelby, Marshall Zelaznik, Joe Rogan, Bruce Buffer, Marc Ratner, Joe Silva, Tim O'Toole, Anthony Giordano, Joe Spaulding, Josh Hedges, Leslie Hedges, Liz Hedges, Kim Lynch, Lora Dircz, Loren Mack, Christy King, Rachel Trontel, Beth Turnbull, Michael Mersch, Richie Vadnais, Michelle Watkins, Michelle Goodwin, Chari Cuthbert, Rachel Sutton, Cara Frieden, Tony Barboza, Tom Page, Morgan Towle, Chad Hurley, Diann Brizzolara, Jason Eible, Rachelle Leah, Jackie Poriadjian Arianny Celeste, Edith LaBelle and all the other UFC staff members that helped me on this project.

Michele C. Quinn for her outstanding expertise as curator for the Octagon exhibitions.

Tim Jefferies for the exhibition at Hamiltons Gallery in London.

Christophe Van De Weghe for his exhibition at Van De Weghe Fine Art Gallery in New York.

Dave Hickey for his insightful essay and David Mamet for his beautiful foreword.

Tom Gerbasi for his great writing skills and expertise on this sport.

Mike Degler, Brian Shotton, Mike Vaccaro, David Waybright, Christian Sumner and Keith Lowe from DK Publishing for making this trade edition book.

Craig Cohen and Daniel Power from powerHouse Books for making the oversized Octagon book and taking it on in the early stages.

Mine Suda for designing this beautiful book.

My mentor Greg Gorman for all the years of friendship, travel, and photographic knowledge he has given to me.

Al Hunter, Ben Granados, and Toby Blue from Petrol Advertising for introducing me to the UFC and helping me make this book.

Andris Lukjanovics, my loyal and dedicated assistant, for always inspiring me with his hard work and great disposition.

Lucy Gallardo, Patrick Lewis, Melissa Smith, Susy Herrera, Lori Nelson, Craig Pilgian, Nicole Moffatt, Russell Roberts, Mike Casciello, Lynne Nerenbaum, Kevin Pontuti, Dominiquie Vandenberg, Stefan Kaluza, Claudia Rogge, Reiner Opoku, Thomas Druyen, Horst Wackerbarth, Bonnie Werth, Jim McCune, Greg Daly, Brian Diamond, Leah Overstreet, Todd Ames, Dave Schwarz, Salil Gulati, Terry Minogue, Michael Levine, Milinda Zumpano, Jonathan and Gabi Frank, Michael Eisner, Angela Krass, Cindy Adkins, Richard Marchisotto, Monna Lee, Lisa Martinez, Mattias and Jenna Segerholt, Steph and Leslie Sebbag, John Sabel, Tanja Paajanen, Idi Gondelman, Richard Sanchez, David Ikeda, Gayle Means, Philippe Poezach, Danny Robinson, Hylton Lea, Jan, Amy and Benjamin Ebeling, Kim Biggs, Alan Bess, Dennis Keeley, Everard Williams Jr., Steve Simmons, David Fahey, Nick Fahey, Christian Poulsen, Tom Oleson, , Jack Showalter, Jeff Payne Mark Duhaime, Bruce Wiseman, Jim Chaconas, Frank and Maria Gargani, Mel Kadel, Brent Langdon, Sergio Ortiz, Damon Lobel, David Schrumpf, Matt Fuss, Ross Morrison, Ronn Brown, Stowe Richards, Tristan Fitzpatrick, Randy Redekopp, Michael Roach, Rod Dyer, Craig Waltcher, Alli Cope, Paul Segan, Trish Swords, Geraldo De La Paz, Richie Knapp, David Ambrose, Jean-Marc Vlaminck, Mandee Johnson, Shotsie Kramer, Louis Lidik, my Italian Agents, Paolo Disca and Monica Provezza at BLOB, Kimberly Feldman-Ayl and Jonathan Feldman at ICON and my agents Bruce Kramer, Giselle Keller, Bill McClure, Suzanne Siriotis and Stephanie Baptist at Artmix Photography.

Heartfelt thanks to my best friend, Luca Giorgetti, for always being in my corner.

My family: Hillary Young, Luca, Nick, Lilo, Jacky and Marvin Lynch, Barbara, Sanford, Gerrit and Brelis Young, and Sydney, Maya and Brian Eisner.

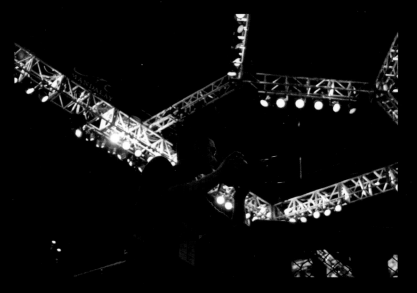

DK/BradyGames, a division of Penguin Group (USA) Inc.
800 East 96th Street, 3rd Floor
Indianapolis, IN 46240

Library of Congress Cataloging-in-Publication Data:
Lynch, Kevin.

Octagon: photographs/by Kevin Lynch.

ISBN: 978-075664563-2

Art direction by Kevin Lynch and Mine Suda
Book design by Mine Suda
Adapted for trade by Keith Lowe

For more information on the UFC, please visit www.ufc.com

10 9 8 7 6 5 4 3 2 1

Printed and bound in China

ARTIN FABIANO SCHERNER DEAN LISTER STEPHAN BONN

MARK WEIR PHILLIP MILLER VLADIMIR MATYUSHENKO A

CHUCK LIDDELL FALANIKO VITALE IAN FREEMA

VIT TANK ABBOTT KIMO LEOPOLDO KARO

MAN GEORGES ST. PIERRE WES SIMS MIKE

N LAMBERT IVAN MENJIVAR JAY HIERON KEN SHAM

PHIL BARONI MATT HUGHES CHRIS LEBEN DA

OSH THOMSON RONALD JHUN TONY FRYKLUND RASH

KE KYLE FORREST GRIFFIN JUSTIN EILERS DENN

ASON DENT SHERMAN PENDERGARST JOSH KOSC

THIAGO ALVES IVAN SALAVERRY JORGE RIVERA

ATO VERISSIMO GIDEON RAY QUINTON JACKSON

MACHIDA LYOTO FRANK TRIGG EVAN TANN

ARCIO CRUZ PATRICK COTE BRANDON VERA DI

ROGER HUERTA SAM HOGER KEITA NAKAMURA

JASON THACKER MIKE SWICK DIEGO SANCHEZ B

ANDERSON SILVA TRAVIS LUTTER ALEX KARAL

LODUNE SINCAID LOGAN CLARK JAKE O'BRIEN GA

RANDY COUTURE MIKE VAN ARSDALE ALESSIO SAKARA

AMPMANN FRANK EDGAR JEREMY HORN JEREMY JACKSO